SENTINEL OF THE HIMALAYAS

Colonel Chhewang Rinchen, MVC & Bar, SM

SENTINEL OF THE HIMALAYAS

Colonel Chhewang Rinchen, MVC & Bar, SM

KIRAN BHOLE
RUPAM CHANDRA ROY

PRABHAT
PRAKASHAN

Published by
PRABHAT PRAKASHAN PVT. LTD.
4/19 Asaf Ali Road,
New Delhi-110 002 (INDIA)
e-mail: prabhatbooks@gmail.com

ISBN 978-93-5562-236-5

SENTINEL OF THE HIMALAYAS
Colonel Chewang Rinchen, MVC & Bar, SM
by Kiran Bhole & Rupam Chandra Roy

Foreword by Colonel Sonam Wangchuk, MVC

Photos Credit: Indian Army & Ladakh Scouts, provided by Dr Phunsog Angmo

Cover designed by Roshan Kumar

Edition
First, 2024

Price
₹ 450 (Rupees Four Hundred Fifty Only)

Printed at
Sita Fine Arts, Delhi

“अङ्‌णवेदी वसुधा कुल्या जलधिः स्थली च पातालम् ।
वल्मीकश्च सुमेरूः कृतप्रतिज्ञस्य वीरस्य ।”

(For a warrior with a pledge and conviction, the world looks like a park, violent oceans seem mere canals, the underworld (Patala) is just like a small ground, and the mighty Mount Sumeru is nothing more than an ant hill.)

– ***Harshacharitram** 7.1*

Dedication

Our work is dedicated to all unsung heroes, units, battalions, and regiments of Indian Army who defended us since awakening of this nation.

Foreword

The name of Col. Rinchen evokes a myriad of sentiments for his rich and valiant soldier's life. His services in the defence of the union territory of Ladakh for the nation are an enviable legacy which only a few are destined to write. Col. Rinchen was born in an epoch, when the country was undergoing the most challenging times and its destiny was being created by the sheer will and sacrifices of some of its greatest sons and daughters. In this tryst with destiny which the nation was exposed to a colossal human tragedy immediately after independence brought about by hatred, fear, and mistrust. This could only be possibly bred by communal frenzy and riots, set to unfold in the form of aggressive designs of a fledgling Pakistan to annex Kashmir by sending in waves of marauders and looters fully supported and sponsored by its armed forces. In this backdrop a young boy rose to stem the portion of this tide of Pakistani invaders in Ladakh. A boy, barely out of his teens led the calling with a handful of local volunteers to defend the vulnerable borders of Nubra Valley, a part of North Ladakh. The boy was none other than late Col. Chhewang Rinchen, youngest receipient Mahavir Chakra Sena Medal, who also fondly came to be known as "The Tiger of Nubra." His saga of valour and courage does not end here, as his heroic deeds towards safe guarding the frontiers of this region and the nation are extensive, spanning four wars with India's sworn enemies on its borders.

The boy was destined to become a great warrior and a true son to his motherland, expert at high altitude warfare and fuelled by a will of fire and courage rarely seen in the annals of the battlefield. Despite his lack of formal military training, the raw courage, grit and dare devilry he displayed in the course of military operations in his long span of soldiering is intriguing. ***Sentinel of the Himalayas*** is the story of the making of a soldier nonpareil, leading the potential readers through his simple childhood and upbringing in a spiritual land where faith and compassion are intrinsic to life. However, should any invader cast at their evil eyes towards this surreal land, their sons and daughters rose to its defence unbeckoned, as valour and ruggedness are the essentials of survival in this unforgiving terrain, for those who are weak at heart would not see the light of the day. His story is a befitting narration for the younger generation of today to emulate, if they ever choose to don the uniform to serve the nation and even otherwise. The bench-mark set by this towering soldier is a calling for every citizen, who resonates with our unique syncretic civilisation.

– Colonel Sonam Wangchuk (Retired), MVC.

A Note From Hero's Daughter

My father late Col Chhewang Rinchen MVC(BAR, SM),was just a student of high school at the age of 17 yrs when he was the 1st to volunteer to push back the Pak invaders who had reached the interior of Nubra in 1947–48. He organized a band of locals (Nubra guards) and held the enemy at bay for 1 months and 23 days, till the regular army came.

For his act of bravery the government inducted him in the army as a Jemadar (Nb subedar). He was awarded the prestigious MVC post facto, thus being the youngest recipient of MVC in the Indian Army. After this there was no looking back. He took up the responsibility of guarding the frontiers and took part in all wars of post independence India.

During the 1962 Indo China War, he fought valiantly on the eastern border and was awarded Sena medal.

In 1965, he was mentioned in dispatches during the Indo pak war. Finally during the 1971 Indo Pak War, he led his forces to recapture Turtuk, Tiakshi, Chalunka, Thang and the surrounding villages, comprising 804 Sq km from the enemy country into the Indian side.

In recognition of his exemplary bravery, the Government awarded him with 2nd MVC, one of the 6 Indian Army officers to be honoured so far.

His love and dedication for the nation goes beyond the call of duty, and an inspiration for generations to come.

Being the eldest of the six progeny of this great warrior soldier I feel great pride and gratitude that Mr.Rupam Roy and Mr.Kiran Bhole are writing his biography. My best wishes are with them.

– Dr. Phunsog Angmo

Author's Note

यो वै भूमा तत्सुखं नाल्पे सुखमस्ति भूमैव सुखं भूमा त्वेव विजिज्ञासितव्य इति भूमानं भगवो विजिज्ञास इति ॥ ७.२३.१ ॥

(Infinity is the source of happiness. There is no happiness in the finite. Happiness can only be found in infinity. But one must try to truly understand what the infinite is.')

– Chandogya Upanishad, Verse 7.23.1.

Reflecting on this pious shloka, our true understanding of Infinity began in the crumbling times of lockdown during the last months of 2020 when the COVID-19 pandemic prevailed across our nation. Rupam, on one usual day, called me with this thought of penning a novel on military subject, he talked about the same context since day one when we became friends. Finally, he woke up with the thought of making up mind and he initiated the search of someone who could be the instrumental note that we were missing in manifesting his idea. He asked me to provide contact of someone who could be interested in the work; for a few weeks we tried to contact people in our circle to lend hand. However, after a long and tedious roll up in contacts, we failed to come across that someone who could be a part of the project. Later he beseeched me to come on-board, to be honest it was scary moment for me and literally a behemoth task. Somehow, I got the spark to agree to sail on the same boat with him, actually my younger sister convinced me to do it. We both have been exhilarating enthusiasts of military and defence domain with unfathomable affection for Indian Armed Forces.

Rupam was a devoted and pious NCC cadet, with a distinctive governor's medal conferred to him and he was mentored by the finest war veterans such as Colonel Gurpreet Singh, SM (Retd), Colonel Balraj Gurung, SM (Retd) and Brigadier Deep Bhagat, SM (Retd). Meanwhile, I was just a weapon and military aficionado. We have been pals since 2018. We have heard about Col. Chhewang Rinchen's persevering life in short and how he is an incredible hero of Ladakh and the finest soldier of Indian Army's golden history. Yet his name was not much resonated around in the mainland. It seemed his deeds and extraordinary service to nation lost somewhere in the winds of time, except in the memories of a handful of army community in the Northern Command.

It was Rupam's intent to write his life chronicles at first, and at that very moment, we decided to bring the story in front of today's generation. We are neither professional novelists nor military historians to be qualified to write a book on such intrepid legend. But we poured our honest toil, heart, mind, time, and soul to produce this fine piece. our true aspiration was to comprehend his indomitable bravery and his life through the days of past and present of Indian Army and to pave a path to our nation's history to explicate the journey of a few incredible people who stood tall to defend our borders. The book is written in the most transparent ways to picturise the life and characteristics of Col. Chhewang Rinchen, especially his understanding, perception of life and his humble military service spanned across four major wars he had served. With a dialogue and definite narrative style, we tried to beget a beautiful picture based on his chronicles from his teen curious years to the brave gentleman who earned MVC at the age of 16 to the warrior who understood the infinity of life during his service and commanded the troops to defend his homeland.

It was truly tough to elaborate and expound with a little information on hand, but Dr.Phunsog Angmo Ma'am, the eldest daughter of Col.Chhewang Rinchen, helped us through thoroughly to achieve this feat. With her guidance and blessing, we finally brought a readable story in front of our readers. Further, our work was refined sheerly by Mrs.Vanaparvathi Siva through her great literature skills, Our team was incomplete without her in these four years journey. We tried our best to do justice with Col.Chhewang Rinchen's valiant name. During this journey, we had real glimpse what infinity truly meant. Serving for a colossal purpose charters the soul to infinity where one truly finds blissfulness, apparently, Col.Chhewang Rinchen's life is a paradigm for it.

Our sources are the experiences that were shared by the kith and kin of Col.Chhewang Rinchen, MVC&BAR, SM, and anecdotes that were narrated by the men who had been with Col. Rinchen during his tenure in the Army. Therefore, we expounded and compartmentalised their experience into narration.

❑

Deepest Gratitude

Gratitude is not just a feeling but an emotion of soul. So, we would like you to know it is overwhelming for us to pen down this note!

Deepest gratitude to our guiding lights for inspiring us to carve the words of history on the pages.

Retired Colonel Sonam Wangchuk, MVC.

&

Dr. Phunsog Angmo.

The book would have stayed only in our minds if Col. Sonam Sir and Dr. Phunsog Ma'am hadn't stepped in. It became probable with their persevering help and great share of guidance. Besides, they shed light on our gloomy days when we found ourselves last amid the perplexed notions.

It is our accolade to have the foreword from Col. Sonam Sir who boosts our morale with his wisdom. Retired Colonel Sonam Wangchuk, MVC, is a decorated Kargil War Hero and living legend. His valiant service to nation had earned him great distinction during and after his tenure, especially he is a recipient of Mahavir Chakra, India's second highest gallantry award in Armed Forces. He is a great inspiration to all. We thank him with all our heart and soul.

Dr.Phunsog Ma'am's constant guidance and insight are the reasons we could able to bring this beautiful work to a defined form, It's our fortune that Ma'am assisted us in our work with kindness and patience for four long years. Dr.Phunsog Angmo Ma'am is the eldest daughter of Late Colonel Chhewang Rinchen, MVC&BAR, SM. She is a celebrated doctor with vast experience in the medical field and acclaimed personality in Indian Army fraternity.

Highest and deepest gratitude to Sir and Ma'am.

JAI HIND.

❑

Acknowledgments

The book would have been just some rookie writers' lifetime ambition without some special people who have been standing with us with all they got. Our greatest thanks to our bosom friend, shining wing and major contributor of our book, Mrs Vanaparvathi Siva. Honestly, without her, the book was far from getting completed and compartmentalised. She had been there every time we dialled and pinged to clarify things. With her skills, she refined our literary work to its highest quality with brilliant illustration. Without her touch, our biography would have been in crude form, our team is incomplete without her. It would be right to say that this book had three authors with her inclusion.

I was obviously reluctant to involve myself in this work but it was my lovable younger sister, Sainidhi Subhash (Iyer) who convinced me to get it done, thanking her with words wouldn't be enough ever for giving me hope and believing in me. She became the pillar of my strength when I tussled to navigate through sources, she kept me determined on this cause and acted as a guiding light whenever I needed her. Moreover, I also desire to thank my Jeeju (brother-in-law), Major Subhash Kumar, for his constant support and insight with caring words, one of my big inspiration. Further, we like to express our gratitude to Mr. Deepak Surana, a famed and talented military novelist. He needs no introduction in the military genre. His unwavering support and guidance to Rupam was the reason we began this incredible journey. And, our sincere thanks to Mr. Jai Samota, who shared his profound perception in our work, he himself is a great writer on defence and military. We further thanks to Mrs. Adrija Sen ma'am for helping us during our initial days of writing.

With heavy heart, we remember and perceive the two legends of Indian Army, Late Lieutenant Colonel Shashi Anand, and Late Havildar Tashi Motup whom we lost two years ago. Late Lieutenant Colonel Shashi Anand of 1 Maratha Light Infantry (Jangi Paltan) passed away on 26th August 2021 after his long battle with ailment. During the 1971 War, Shashi sir was attached to Ladakh Scouts and was tasked to defend the Karakoram Pass from enemy advances. With his brave Ladakhi men, he successfully defended the area from the Pakistan Army's Karakoram Guards.

Shashi sir was one of the Nonnos (Brother) of Colonel Chhewang Rinchen, MVC**, SM served the Ladakh Scouts from 1971 to 1974 as an Adjutant. We are forever grateful for his selfless service. We were fortunate to have an interview when he took us to the days of his past through his words.

We felt blessed to know Late Havildar Tashi Motup who was the only living soldier of the first troop of the Nubra Guards, raised by Colonel Chewang Rinchen, MVC**, SM in 1947. Born in 1929 in Sumur Village, Nubra Valley., during the Indo-Pak War of 1947-1948, at the age of 19, he volunteered for the Nubra Guards to protect his motherland. With just 10 days of training and some ammunition, under the leadership of Colonel Rinchen, he along with the troops became the reason for the adversaries to retreat and held the position for 1 month and 23 days until the support from the Indian Army arrived. After the war, he was enlisted in the Indian Army. He served as the kindest and staunch soldier of the Indian Army. He had participated in four wars and served in many operations since independence. Unfortunately, he departed the world last year at the age of 93 last year. It is our benediction that we had had the chance to interview him a couple of times. He shared the tales of glory and insights about his days with Rinchen sir during service. We are obliged to his great service to the nation.

From the bottom of our hearts, we thank Mr. Tsering Wangchuk, Nephew of Col. Chhewang Rinchen, and son of his only sister Mrs. Phuntsog Angmo who aided us in all the way and brought us an opportunity to have conversation with Havildar Tashi Motup sir who cherished sharing his experience and early days with Rinchen sir. Moreover, we desire to thank, Phuntsog Angmo, the younger sister of Col. Chhewang Rinchen, who has been amiable every time we converse about thoughts and memories she shared with her eldest brother. Without her presence, we would be rendered thin in penning our book.

We are grateful to our alter egos and best buddies, whose endorsement and support holds us in our long cause, Mr.Jecinth Albert, Mr.Aakash Kumar, Ms. Saianshi Mohapatra, Mr.Sachin Kamath, Mr.Umran Shariff, Mr.Soumya Ranjan Mohanty and Mr.Swaraj Kar.

Last of all, we extend our gratitude to our parents and family for believing us. We took a while longer than expected, and everyone has been patient with us, we are indebted to you all.

We wind up with a few lines for our readers who has been in our thought since the day the book bloomed in our imagination. Friends, it is neither a story of 'many moons ago' or 'once upon a time' but an epic which has story of a man and his comrades who gave everything that he adored to the nation. Let us respect the soldiers not only when they arrive in coffin!

❑

Contents

Chapter I

How It All Began

Ldumra, widely known as the 'Valley of Flowers' by the ethnic groups of the terrain, is a serene valley where history can be traced back to the initial defence strategies of India in 1947 when the nations' independence bloomed with conflicts to tackle. When the other parts of India gathered themselves to sign the pacts and memorandums, there was an agreement signed with blood and sweat.

Ldumra, which scatters the fragrance of myriad of flowers on the towering hills in the lap of Karakoram Range like a lawn of green oasis in sand dunes and snow desert, wears its scars from the yesteryears with pride to narrate a story to everyone whoever steps on the land. It is located above the crown of India, with a burst of mighty sunshine over the enchanting valley in Western Ladakh. The world recognises it as "Nubra Valley", which is opposite to the locally called name "Ldumra." It is situated downrange from the Siachen glacier and begets the Nubra River, the lifeline of the Valley and extremely close to Gilgit-Baltistan westward.

In the map of India, Ldumra is a place with captivating sights which were preserved once, by the bravest souls who stood in the frontiers to guard, in the earliest stage of invasion, after independence. Whenever the breeze crosses Ldumra, it touches the soil to smell the valiant epic of a man who was born and brought up along the river side of the hamlet, Sumur. He later grew up to be the finest warrior whose contribution were written in the pages of history of the Indian Army's that how his devoted involvement enabled to draw the map of India with a crown.

More fascinating than fantasies and ballads, the Nubra river flows with ample anecdotes. Just down the Nubra river lies the Sumur village with the bequest of its continuous service in defending Ladakh since medieval times with its unique history of raising warriors to defend the land against enemy frontiers. The hamlet, which is a humble husk of Tibetan Buddhist people living in harmony, has the loudest pride of Indian forces, the mighty mountains of Siachen, the peaks where the Indian Army carried out Operation Meghdoot to take over the glacier in a pre-emptive strike. Now, at an elevation of 10,157 feet, Sumur breathes in harmony and hums the history to the Transhimalayan mountain range to spread it to the world.

Today, the world's highest military point is officially a part of India. This became possible with the selfless escapades of the snow warriors of Ladakh, who were the first to climb and conquer the mountains of Siachen Glacier with the Kumaon Regiment as a part of an operation in 1984. The Ladakh Scouts have had an outstanding record of service even before its inception. Adding the valour of narratives, the story of a tiny hamlet, Sumur village, widens with an additional pride of carrying a snow warrior in its womb without foretelling the fate of the boy who, later, became the reason for the freedom of Nubra Valley. His umpteen endeavours in the line of duty were witnessed by the Indian Army in the captivating Himalayan Ranges since 1947.

Remembering him as the progenitor of Ladakh Scouts and stoic revered Man of the Gallantry, or Tiger of Nubra are one of the soul-filling ways to remember his legacy of courage and perseverance. His life ensembles the heroic deeds which showcases Nubra Valley being an adobe of picturesque settlement with lavish green fields. He was the embodiment of the glories that Ladakh region had seen while defending the presence of adversaries on the forehead of our motherland. He was born as a common man who had equipped himself for the oath he took. His name is associated with surplus memories and moments of bravery without which the pages of history from 1947 to 1971 would have been different. The man was Colonel Chhewang Rinchen, MVC & Bar, SM, extensively known as the "Stak of Ldum ra" (Tiger of Nubra).

Tuesday, January 15, 1992

The day commenced with an immersed delight as the Indian Army Day was being celebrated. The wind blew with the spirit of patriotism in every nook and corner of India. So did the dazzled atop Leh too, the regimental centre of the Ladakh Scouts. When the heroes of Ladakh Scouts were being remembered during the invincible day on the ground of Phyang with the conversations of new recruits of the unit. Approximately 117 km away from the base a lone and calm whisper of Nubra's tiger, in the nest of snow warriors in alleyways of Sumur village, echoed in the Trans-Himalayan range. He soaked himself in the waves of reminiscence.

It was a hazy and cloudy day in the mid-January as the temperature reached below zero degrees Celsius on an average scale in the valley. The people were swamped with their days inside the Huts, in the misty winter, with their household chores. The mornings in the cradle of Nubra's dunes were filled with distinct fragrance and scenery, especially the village Sumur which was a reason for him to walk through the trails. The bank of Yarma Tsangpo, locally called as Nubra river, gave him the sights of past. At the ripe age of 60, then retired, Col. Chhewang Rinchen often strolled through the pathways calmly and with a gentle smile on his face and absorbing the day-to-day life of the villagers. He was self-contained with his grasping presence while crossing through lanes surrounded by old huts and homes of Sumur where the villagers had great reverence for him.

Not only for being a war hero of the land, he is remembered in the village even now for limitless reasons, the notable ones are his personality of great etiquettes and the humbleness he exhibited towards everyone even though he belonged to the most reputable family. He earned the respect through his deeds and social behaviour. People of the village admired the connection between him and the land which was always inseparable and inevitable. He always treated the village as his family, which was the reason his compelling and eloquent aura used to be felt whenever he wandered even now where ever he had wandered. Even though he lived in Leh, he used to visit sumur to meet his dear mother and his people occasionally at his birthplace and relived his nostalgic memories with them.

Once, while walking across a few villagers with a radio caught his attention in the corner of the street. The All India Radio broadcasting was a nominal choice in the remote villages on the borderline of India. Despite being close to the Tibetan language, the Ladakhi population had a good understanding of languages such as Hindi and Urdu. When Col.Chhewang Rinchen was crossing the group of villagers mild humming of the national anthem fell onto his ears. It was the Indian Army Day and Prasar Bharti was delivering the news regarding the celebration of the historic event. A nostalgic vibe surged in his eyes looking for his days in the Army that made him a little dense with echoing thoughts of past. To be precise, 117 kms away from the Ladakh Scouts, the memories of a warrior merged with the wind which gusted with patriotism.

The man with the heart of steel had a wave of flashbacks striking his mind. It was neither the first nor the last time since he unlocked his service days from memories. While he deeply drowned in his thoughts, he didn't forget to notice the villagers; the instinct of a soldier was alert as always. A gentle smile was delivered to the middle-aged group of men who were standing with the radio. It took them a minute to realise that the living soul of patriotism just sauntered in the path after standing for a mere fraction of minutes beside them. They watched him stroll away and that silhouette of moment served as a testament for his strong character. Those villagers had cherished the couple of minutes of his presence even after he left the spot.

As he had kept walking, he suddenly stopped at a place where all the answers for his heavy memories were preserved in petals, his dilapidated primary school in the village. The young fire-willed Chhewang Rinchen had lived his blazing days in the premises during his childhood which returned to be a bunch of memories for him to much when the face shimmered with wrinkles of experience. The school and the ground had the front pages of the epic which were written by its one of the pupils later. Five decades ago, the school had nurtured the young Chhewang who dreamt of serving the nation. It was not novel for him to visit his alma mater; the place that built his base from where he emerged with determination in heart and indomitable thoughts in his mind.

The children's favourite and village's honourable personage had his own distinctive habits while going to his alma mater. Bringing toffees for the school children was his favourite routine.

Indeed! The children just knew with the first glimpse when he ought to set foot into the school premises that he had toffees with him for them. As Chhewang Rinchen's nephew was studying in the same school, he had a habit of getting around at school every day to meet children and having a good time around the campus. The school had the significance of sharpening young Rinchen with virtues and good values who transformed himself as a finest gentleman. Besides, he had become the icon of the school and had set the limits high for the future pupils.

He spent his primary schooling days as a young blooming soul unknown to his future, a devout Buddhist, influenced by harmony, humbleness, and modesty in his early childhood before heading to Leh for higher studies. The school had strengthened his foundation for a journey which would require the greatest willpower and self-esteem later.

The children from the school cherished seeing him bringing toffees, including his nephew, which itself was a joyful moment for him. They came outside like flocks of smiling cubs and in a flash, the toffees were in their little white palms, the spark in the eyes of those small kids while eating the sweet candies was what used to make his entire day, when he returned from the path of defending and offending.

While the children venturing their playful and innocent acts in break time, Col. Rinchen relaxed for a while in the surroundings where once he had also played and studied with his brothers. Looking at the kids was a worthy visit for him. As a father of five daughters and a son, he was always a family-oriented person who was fond of having kids around. However, the moments he relished with the children were also a part of the journey he created in his life that he had sacrificed decades to earn the blissfulness of peace. The young generation of the village had been safe and fortunately living life in tranquillity without knowing that Col. Rinchen didn't just bring toffees but also the sweetness of safety.

As dusk starts from the west, Col. Rinchen returned to his path saying bye to the cubs. While returning "I want to be like you one day" was heard, before he could see his face, the kid vanished in the throng of students who were rushing inside the school. Though he failed to identify the face, his heart felt a bit of bliss. The reputation and will of fire Chhewang Rinchen had created in the souls of people of the village was palpable through various incidents like this. It was his legacy, certainly!

The words pierced his heart, however, it also impaled the core of history.

Tossed in baffled thoughts, Chhewang Rinchen returned to his home, ‘The Stakre House’ as the name of his residence would reflect the spark of history as the name was given to Rinchen’s house by the villagers. Stak means 'Tiger' and Stakre House means “Tiger's House”. The name was bestowed by Gyalpo (King) of Ladakh during the 1830s to Chhewang Rinchen’s great grandfather due to his valour displayed in defending Ladakh during a battle with forces of turk invader Mirza Haider. His family commanded a great history of bravery and later, Chhewang Rinchen became the modern symbol of it as the tiger’s name continued to be on his crest as part of his will and determination. He was called the ‘Tiger of Nubra’ for no less reasons.

The Stakre House has been a living symbolism of bravery in Sumur village even now.

The light of the day was settling down, the temperature in the village dropped drastically to an extreme low, but the villagers were quite solid with the high mountainous temperature drops as they had been having the benediction of the land, tolerant to extreme weathers. Nubra Valley witnesses -14°C as its average night temperature.

In the frozen nightfall, he sat beside the burning bonfire with the most trusted buddy a soldier could have in his solitude. The old monk was the signature choice of any battle-hardened soldier, the retired Colonel who had seen four wars in his 37 years of military tenure surely knew the true companion of his memories. Every sip tasted better with golden memories. The warmth of rum in the chilling night alongside the bonfire evoked the legacy of yesteryears. Besides, the mountains too, whispered the honour of his days in uniform, his cheerful and blazing eyes unknowingly turned into a dense mirror of the old times. Without no reason, it is not being said “There is always a battle left in you for yourself.”

With every drop of reminiscence, the rum continued to slide down through his throat and his mind slowly immersed in voices and visuals of the early innocent days in the school. With the surreal tunes were drumming, he began to remember the time when he used to play with his siblings. The summit around used to reverberate with the melody of drums and flutes he played in the past.

As the emotions drizzled more in-depth, his breath reignited with enormous grit while remembering the glorious in military service. Every person in the village and neighbouring villages knew the history of the legend who defended the valley with 28 groups of guards for months against the mounting enemy from the west. Every single dreaming child in the village heard of his heroic times, but every hero of war is often outspoken during solitude. The soliloquy was what every veteran experiences during lonely nights. Without exception, Col. Rinchen's vast service in the field caught up with him and the memories of the horrors of war every time he would sit by himself.

The man, for whom the wars were effortless to fight, was battling with time, when the uniform became his memory, in every breath he too. When the chilly night embraced his loneliness, every flip of his eyebrows took him back to his days, to his struggles, to the coffins carried, to the excruciating paths, to his pains, to his adventures, to his achievements, to his chronicles, to his will of stoicism. He had been in his early teenagehood when he was honoured with India's second-highest wartime gallantry award, Mahavir Chakra, making him the youngest MVC recipient at the age of 17 for his heroic lead and contribution in defending the Nubra Valley and capturing enemy strongholds while pushing them nearly 50 km behind. The record went on, to be repeated, as he was inducted into the Indian Army officially at a relatively young age. These accolades were just a memoir for a soldier who committed more actions beyond the times with an inextinguishable will. It was the desire to serve the land with all his heart.

Col. Rinchen had dedicated more than half of his life to serve in the Indian Army. He was engulfed by the mind filling echoes of war cries, slogans, burst of rifles, scream of enemies and, most of all, undying breath of his companions who stood beside him till the last brick of stronghold to protect even the last inch of the land that they defended together with sheer will and robust determination. The pain and the pleasure were tangled in his memories. Elated laughter and a droplet at the corner of eyes in the remembrance of such bittersweet memory. Further, he continued dissolving every drop of his drink in the depth of his memories of devout service towards the motherland.

The question remains the same in the journey of his life. It is necessary to be asked by someone who is curious about how the young fire-willed Chhewang Rinchen conquered the pinnacle and became the 'Tiger of Nubra' who is recognised as the great hero of Ladakh even today.

As Col. Rinchen relaxed pondering over his glorious days flashing before his eyes while embracing himself, the answer to the question "How did it all begin?" begins here, for the readers, in a profound manner.

❑

Chapter 2

A Young Cub in the Valley

Clippers of chilling wind could be heard whistling, like mountains composing honied tunes in the valley. The sky heralded extreme winter and a hazy view around the region was palpable. A white blanket covering the hamlet of Sumur looked like nature wanted to play hide and seek with days and nights. Vaguely in heart but crisp in mind, slowly the memories evaded his eyes.

It was mid-April in 1941, The sharp noon worried none. A puzzled young Chhewang was standing with his young brother before the steep hill. Roughly at the age of ten, Rinchen and his four-year-old younger brother Phuntsog Namgial were waiting for their friends to gather at the bottom of the hill. It was a beautiful afternoon on the weekend. The sun was shining bright clocking the day's summertime at peak and the young cubs of Sumur were excited to race, setting the peak as destination.

An ardent son and amiable elder brother, Chhewang Rinchen always had an upright audacity and wise nature since his childhood. His lifeline was rooted to his friends and family. Chhewang Rinchen's four friends arrived to the spot and looked straight up. Without any reluctance, all six kids had started climbing the hill at once. The blooming smiles on their faces turned into a face filled with determination to touch the hilltop. Eventually, descending with high spirits like dusty cubs who never got fatigued. Only a man who lives his life to the fullest would have something to much, so did the retired Chhewang Rinchen.

Young Rinchen was known to be a remarkable and humble child. He was said to be born on an auspicious day according to the Ladakhi calendar belonging to the year of the horse. It was the 15th day of the year which can be angled on 11th November 1931 on the Georgian calendar. Chhewang Rinchen is the eldest son of Kunzang Dorje and Jamyang Dolma, a reputable family and the name bearer of Stakre Lineage. Rinchen's father Kunzang Dorje was a watcher and sentinel to the vast valley around the village, on behalf of Kalon of Ladakh who was descendant of the Prime Minister to Ladakh's Raja in the early 19th century.

His childhood was replete with tale of mischief in the pure innocence. When the kids were sliding through the sand peaks of the hill, they soon lost track of time in their delightful play. The dusk dispersed the day while Rinchen realised that the next day, he had to visit his spiritual teacher in gompa and later to missionary master Stanzin. He grabbed his little brother's hand and stormed with exhilarating breath towards his house, waving a hasty bye to his playmates.

Though young, he had the awareness of spiritual learning. He knew the value of spiritual learning which led him to respect and revere his spiritual master. He was a child who believed in the compassion of people. Besides, he devoted himself for the philosophy of Buddha. However, destiny was waiting for him with a mantle of soldier in the far land of Leh ahead in future. Unaware of time's course, a humble student of local primary school and follower of Samstanling Gompa returned home with his brother that evening. The smile on their mother's face welcomed them. Samstanling was a famous holy monastery (Gompa) on the revered mountain peak adjacent to the village, with the heights of

3050 metres. It was a home for several hundred Ladakhi Lamas and Chomos who would follow the Tibetan sect of Buddhism. Chhewang Rinchen had spent his few years of cultural studies visiting in the Gompa beside studying in local school situated in village.

Hailing from one of the dignified and devout Buddhist families, the values of Rinchen's house had beliefs in compassionate peaceful notions. Rinchen had three brothers, Phuntsog Nyamgial, Sonam Dorje and C. Norbu with a young sister named Phuntsog Angmo, All four siblings were known to inherit the virtues from their parents. Rinchen's father Kunzang vested his early days in travelling deep in Northern Tibet for trade purposes despite being an ardent farmer. Occasionally, Kunzang and his wife, had travelled to Lhasa carrying Sattu, Atta and Apricot in return importing Chinese porcelain, carpet, and tea.

The chilly atmosphere of the Tibetan region made tea a lucrative beverage for the local people. Sumur village sits in the cradle of river confluence with the mighty Himalayas gazing upon the land making the region a basket of the winters. Thus, tea was the bond shared between the Ladakhi and Tibetan people.

Rinchen inherited the exploration instinct from his father, regularly surfing through the time and hilltops of the valley, ardently visiting to Lamas in Gompa, reverend master Stanzin and attending primary school in village. Silent yet obedient to his own accepting nature, Chhewang Rinchen spent his primary schooling days seeking spiritual sermons and honing his positivity under multiple spiritual teachings with a hope to explore the outer boundaries of the valley.

In Ladakhi tradition, it is a household culture to send one of the family's children to gompa, in the adolescent stage, so that offered child would become part of bhikshu (Lama) or (Chomo) bhikshuni custom, learning higher Buddhist moral values and prayers for several years under celibacy. Rinchen's father also had spent his adolescent years at the Gompa getting spiritual knowledge and teaching of bhikshu under Buddhist scripture studies before renouncing celibacy and turning into a household man. Unlike his father, Rinchen never had a deep fascination with scripture reading with Lamas, but he had great faith in Lord Buddha and he was spiritual.

"Chhewang, try to return home early before dusk", his mother's voice echoed through the doorstep. "Mother, I returned early today." Chhewang Rinchen whispered, while both siblings rushed home giggling and talking, as their mother took them inside home retelling their names. Names could be common but not the emotions with them.

Chhewang Rinchen's name had a vivid story behind it. It was being said that few months after he was born, the village census was conducted. The person who took the registration on behalf of revenue department for the population count was called "Patwari", when he visited the home of Kunzang Dorje, he witnessed the child was unnamed, that was the same time when Kunzang and his wife entered in the census. So, further to complete the registration Patwari took the liberty of naming and gave him the title of "Chhewang Rinchen" in census list when he had no idea, what this name would become in the future.

Soon after, to comply with Tibetan Buddhist custom, the parents took infant Chhewang to the Lama for a proper name, coincidentally the same name was pronounced in the shrine too. So, the parents considered it as a benediction. The meaning of his name "Hero" in the local dialect didn't add heroism in his life, but he justified a new meaning to the name Chhewang, that is, the man of valour.

The following day, nonchalantly young Rinchen took the road to walk towards his master's house to meet him. Master Stanzin was a missionary and a practising evangelist who lived in the village with his wife. He was a tranquil and demeanour personality, one of the profound souls that had a great influence on Rinchen's early emerging days.

"You took a while!", Master uttered, "I saw some village youngsters going out of the village, so", Rinchen replied.

"So?", Master patiently looked at him.

"So, I wondered, will there be a time I too have to go?" Rinchen's eyes had the deep thoughts.

"It depends," Master voiced while placing his hand on young Rinchen's head.

"Depends on what Master?" the tiny eyes asked.

"On what purpose, you serve to step out." He quoted simply. "I don't have any purpose now." curious Rinchen expressed.

"You'll find your purpose one day, maybe not here but out there someday. Just have faith." The master's words satisfied his quest. Young Chhewang nodded with a smile and focused on what his master had taught.

Master Stanzin's preaching smoothly engulfed the mind of young Rinchen, no wonder that Rinchen's finest acts were rooted with the words of his master.

As days were crawling, the string of time presented him surplus chances to dig in and drown deep. His mind started to take shape under several influences. Rinchen, in his teenage years, took interest in painting, with the mindset of a child who desired to try everything in the world. It was an imagery imprint of his Venerable Lama in Sumur Village whose inspiration ushered an artistic urge in him slowly.

Art had a profound effect on young Rinchen's life. His visionary command of intricating adaptability in shape and colours of his surroundings while painting a certain object was archetypal. Fascinated, young Rinchen projected cavernous interest in drawing. Specially meditating Lord Buddha cast a moral impression on him in later days. He took lessons for painting from his lama of Sumur village. While learning to paint, he developed interest and learnt the skill of sculpting too.

Rinchen had a unique habit. He used to accomplish responsibilities in devotional ways. He knew the importance of completing the tiny daily works in a dedicated manner. It is pointless to say more about who and what he was even when he was a child.

"Om Mani Padme Hum, Om Mani Padme Hum, Om Mani Padme Hum '', the holy chant commenced with the rise of the day. As the mantra had scattered in the wind all the villagers reverberated with the first chant of the sacred words with the opening light of the day hitting the Samstanling Gompa and later immersed the entire village. The wind continued chanting which was heard by every ear, Young Rinchen caught a bright smile when the chants fell on his eardrums. It was the fourth month of the Tibetan calendar. The auspicious day of the Saka Dawa festival had arrived. It was the day when Sakyamuni Gautama Buddha was born, took his enlightenment, and achieved Nirvana.

Saka Dawa signifies the "Disu month" in the Tibetan language. Disu is one of the 28 astrological constellations of the Tibetan calendar. As Disu appears in the fourth month, it is known as the Disu month, Saka Dawa is also known as Vaishakh or Vesak, a sacred day of the year revered for being holy in Buddhist festivals. On this day, Ladakhi and Tibetan households chant Sutras and sacred chants, offer prayers to Lord Buddha and show compassion to all living beings, for instance, people release the cattle and animals to mark respect for them. The holy monastery in the region changes the flag in the pole to signify the arrival of the auspicious day. The custom still gets followed by the people who carry forward the legacy of the land.

The Samstanling Gompa's flagpole was changed by the holy lamas living there. The village was turned into a humming cradle of sacred hymns. Young Chhewang, after offering litanies to Lord Buddha and receiving blessings from his parents, took his younger brother with some loads of packed things to downtown village grounds. People were outside, cattle and animals were released. Rinchen was brought up amid all these traditions that gave him a purpose in life and he respected the history of the soil.

It was early June in 1942, a small settlement of the village had turned into a dazzling land of festivals. People were selling distinctive handlooms and homemade stuff like a clay pot, clothes, tea, food grains, etc. Young Chhewang was curiously looking for a place and he finally found it. He set up his little stall of sculptures and paintings of Lord Buddha. He sold various items of his handmade art works and earned money at carnivals. How thrilled and blessed his little palms would have felt when the hard-earned money in his hands! Money was more than silver coins when earned with sweat through a truthful path. Rinchen understood that in his emerging stage of life, the Saka Dawa Festival was a piece of his path in which he walked with virtue and visions.

The eldest son of Kunzang reached the end of his primary schooling days. Rinchen's father had a desire to send his son for higher studies. Being a caring father, Kunzang Dorje knew the importance of higher education and it would be impossible for his son to receive it in Sumur village. It was the early days of 1943. The Kalon of Ladakh had visited the village for inspection. The then Kalon Chhewang Rigzin happened to meet Rinchen's father at his home.

Young Rinchen received the elderly guest with great honour. Kunzang beseeched Kalon to allow his son to visit Leh for higher studies. Kalon, who belonged to the family of a then Prime Minister of the Gyalpo of Ladakh was generous towards Kunzang and seeing his hope for Rinchen's bright future, he agreed to take Young Rinchen to Leh.

Rinchen's nerves recalled his conversation with his master. He swallowed his thoughts. He felt that the resolution he had been eager to discover must be away from the village waiting for him to uncover, somewhere in Leh.

Rinchen accepted the decision. However, it was not an easy decision for his mother to accept. Though the love for Rinchen tugged at her heart, she stood with a strong motive of sending Rinchen to an optimum institute. Now, she is revered as "Mother of Nubra" for her motherhood and compassion in the village. Rinchen's mother accepted the decision to send her beloved son to Leh for his higher education.

Before leaving the village, Rinchen rushed to master Stanzin to bid farewell.

"Will I get it there?", he asked.

Master asked, "And what is that?"

"My Purpose, Master." He cleared.

"Your purpose will come to find you, just be who you are," Master said in a clear tone.

Young Rinchen later left with the words of his master in mind. His inclusiveness started to expand his outward strength as he stepped into the new chapter of his life. After bidding farewell to his family, village, and his memories; Rinchen travelled to the heart of Ladakh in the town of Leh with Kalon.

Leh was the northernmost city during the British rule. It was the time of World War II when the allied forces were at peak wartime. In the context of history, Leh was a focal place. The British Indian Army actively participated in all war theatres around the globe. The Indian subcontinent had been in a debacle due to the uprising of the independence movement and wartime causes. Leh acted as the furthermost military garrison for the British Indian Army against northern frontiers. It was an obvious case that the presence of police and military forces were common those days in Leh. It was one of the fundamental contexts under which Young Rinchen was heading to discover a new dimension of life.

Entering Leh, Young Rinchen found a completely different world compared to his village Sumur, which had minimum of people but maximum of the natural setting. Leh was a canvas of steaming studded large settlements people with the first sight of a little buzzing vehicles and Mud Houses at a greater site. It was by far the only known city in the Northern forehead of India, second to Srinagar in Kashmir.

Kalon introduced Young Rinchen to his wife Spaldon and son Rigzin Namgial. Chhewang Rinchen recalled his early days in Leh. Kalon's family was gentle and kind to him. They all welcomed him with open arms.

Kalon had taken care of his living and schooling. He enrolled Rinchen in a high school adjacent to the military ground. The High School was the stepping stone of young Rinchen's upcoming revelation which would propel him to the escapades of military.

One evening, Kalon had invited a few officers for drinks. Being one of the dignitaries of the Leh administration, Kalon was a reputable person around, many administrative officials and military servicemen used to visit him. It was an astonishing moment for Rinchen to see a few men boldly walking with thumping footsteps in uniform. He was fascinated whenever he happened to capture the glimpse of the uniformed men. Curious Rinchen used to observe the officers whenever they visited Kalon. Rinchen was like a part of the Kalon's family since Kalon accepted his responsibility for Rinchen's higher studies.

His heart and mind bustled with excitement and bewilderment every time he looked at the men in uniform. He had various words entangled in his mind. One day, out of intrusiveness, a young scholar Rinchen initiated to interact with the officers. The boldness in his voice impressed the visiting servicemen who also had conversation with him.

"You want to hold it?", a senior officer asked.

Rinchen with a sparkle in his eyes was seeing a service rifle in the hand of a soldier who paid a call on the officer.

"Yes, I want to." a nervous Rinchen replied.

"Don't be a scared child, take it", the officer offered it with care.

Rinchen took the rifle in his hands. Maybe that was the moment when the Army's martial spirit touched his pure heart. For instance, Rinchen took that entire military aura into admiration and accepted the heat of that feeling as part of his liking. Officers admired the young Rinchen and they used to visit Kalon's home. His ears were always alert for news of the heroic events in the war and uncomprehend scenarios which took place during the operations.

The stories of war and actionable events ignited the ember of Rinchen's core ideology. A devout and obedient child who was nurtured in a peaceful and serene village slowly was being equipped by the men in uniform's presence in his life. Leh showed him the path of his inner voice. The patriotism in his blood rushed, the beat of his heat ameliorated the spirit of young Rinchen. The tales he heard and observed took him to the journey in which he found opportunities to explore the martial strength within him.

Witnessing a completely different aspect of the outer world and seeing people who risked their lives to protect the frontiers left a profound impact in his wisdom. Rinchen had spent his early childhood hearing about his ancestors who earned the name "STAK" by defending the region against the invasion of Mongols. The amalgamation of his life's two greatest experiences about selfless service and courage led him towards his life's purpose.

It was just a spark of moment when he finally explored what he was meant for and what his future was. The perseverance in him attracted the entire universe's optimism to get what he desired.

During weekday afternoons, Rinchen used to rush to the end of the square adjacent to the school. The scene he used to witness was exhilarating. It was the dilapidated Leh garrison parade ground where soldiers used to parade, practice basic training, and perform military drills. It was momentarily the best experience for young Rinchen. The visuals and footsteps thumping on the ground were shaping his ideas about his future and his unexplored ambition. Even on holidays, he and his fellow classmates made multiple visits to the ground. Rinchen used to break the ice while interacting with the soldiers asking them vivid questions about their experience.

It was that time when his creativity ushered in a new paradigm. He often wandered around Leh just to witness the mounting of state force officers, aggressive style of operating weapons, loading of rifles, and firing of firearms and guns. He wandered everywhere under the sky to get the sight of uniforms in Leh. The chronicles of bravery, courage and resilience formed a pillar for his true purpose. He had interest in fabricating improvised and simple pistol systems, working ammunition, and complete rifle by salvaged old cartridges, muzzle barrels, bolt rotating piston and much valuable old equipment.

Firing handmade weapons, improvising ammo with available resources and salvaged metal parts were ingrained into his muscle memory. He was already a soldier from the depth of his soul, it was just that one uniform and the rank that was missing. As master Stanzin said, his purpose would find him. Till then he would roam everywhere in Leh to cherish a uniform without knowing the fact that one day that uniform would get honoured because of him.

That martial spirit looming in the breath of Leh had helped young Rinchen to earn his newly ignited will of fire. The serene kid who was the obedient eldest child of a farmer, who practiced the peaceful ordain of Lord Buddha, had turned into a mighty man with determination and purpose. Before turning 15, he had no clue what the future would bring. But the time wheel had its surprise for young Rinchen and India.

❑

Chapter 3

Rising of the Tiger

Destiny was made. Fate was altered. A new saga was approaching the cradle of civilisation. When in other continents, people were nomads, Indians had the glory of scripters and education. Rinchen was 16 years old when he was dreaming to be a part of military forces. He did not know that the upcoming days would demand the best from him and his nation. In the core of Indian landmass, a new chronicle was about to being penned.

The colonial rule exploited the resources when it entered through the Khyber Passage and when the crown departed, it left a permanent scar. Trembling land, scorching sky, and a new era was about to be part of the subcontinent. British Lord Cyril Radcliffe drew his infamous line of partition and divided an ancient prosperous land into three parts. The land was distributed between two newly independent nations, India and Pakistan, on 9th August 1947. Along with independence, India got a rival too. The land of Jammu Kashmir turned into a hotbed soon after. When two countries, India and Pakistan, came into inception, the first War in the subcontinent, after the World War II, broke out.

It was sweltering in the Western frontier of Gilgit which was considered as the last frontier of the Indian stronghold. The region was protected by Gilgit Scouts and was a target zone of Pakistani forces. The subsequent plan by the adversary was to take over the Gilgit stronghold and march towards Skardu which would give entry to Leh through northern boundaries. Brigadier Ghansar Singh was appointed as the Governor of Gilgit and sent to take charge over the post with the right to command the scouts deployed in the region. Due to the Indian Government's goodwill gesture towards the Soviet Union the British supported the Pakistani.

Once again in history, the barbarous strategy of the British, with Pakistan, tricked Gilgit Scouts to cause a coup in the region. Under Major W.A. Brown and Captain Matheson, the troops of Gilgit Scouts revolted on 31 October 1947, by unfurling the Pakistani flag and killing pro Indian troops in response to Maharaja Hari Singh's accession to Indian Union. Brigadier Ghansar Singh was killed in Gilgit and the Siege of Skardu, the prominent city in Gilgit region triggered a war between both the countries on the borders of Jammu Kashmir.

On 1st November 1947, Gilgit was occupied by the Pakistani troops commanded by Col. Aslam Khan with the help of Chitral Scouts under the order of Col. Mata Ul Mulk of Chitral State who acceded to the Pakistani side. Skardu finally fell into the pit after seeing Muslim soldiers advancing. Col. Sher Singh Thapa who later was sent to Skardu fort to defend the region resulted nothing as the local rebel forces had been already influenced by Chitral Scouts, the siege of Skardu Fort had inducted. It was late for the Indian troops to build up against the enemy at Skardu as all region was under the rival troops and their loyalists.

Seeing the pattern of enemy advancement, Brigadier L.P. Sen who was commanding the 161 Infantry Brigade had a serious hunch about the rival's next move. He sensed an attack over Leh in early January 1948. Brigadier Sen proposed his seniors to deploy a small detachment of troops from his Brigade to reinforce the State Forces troops who were guarding Leh. But the response made him feel blue as the reinforcement could be sent only a month later.

At that time Major Prithi Chand (later retired as Colonel) of 2 Dogra assembled a column of about 20 Lahulis and Ladakhis known as X-Force and volunteered to reinforce the state forces. The column left Srinagar on 16 February, 1948. They walked through waist-high snow, faced icy winds over the Zojila route, living mainly on sattu and tea, and reached Leh on 9 March, 1948. The enemy troop was still afar from Leh. Major Prithi Chand was promoted to the rank of Lieutenant Colonel after arriving at Leh. He started raising and training a militia of local villagers.

When the winter in the Karakoram came to an end, the vast snow layers started melting in May that moved the invaders faster and easier. Chorbat La was opened by the enemy on 10 May 1948. Reports arrived soon after that the enemy had gathered in Baidangdo in the Shyok valley. Baidangdo was the second largest village with a population of about 500 Muslims. The route would give access to Leh directly as there was no Indian troops between Skardu and Baidangdo.

After the fall of Kargil on 10 May 1948, the enemy started marching towards Leh in three directions. On 22nd May, the vital bridge Khalatse was taken and soldiers of the State Forces were thrown back by the adversary that most of them were vanished into the neighbouring hills. From Khalatse to Leh, it was only a day-march for the enemy.

Sonam Narboo, the first Ladakhi civil engineer who had completed his engineering abroad came to Leh along with Lt. Col. Prithi Chand. Immediately, after reaching Leh, he started constructing an improvised airstrip along with Babu Dorje. It was the highest airstrip in the world then. Eventually, landing an aircraft on the airstrip was obdurate for the Pilots. The airstrip was T-shaped and runways were only 365 metres and 305 metres. No pilot could land a Dakota aircraft in that airstrip. To make it possible, Air Commodore Mehar Singh volunteered for the impossible task. Major General K.S. Thimaya, GOC of Sri Division decided to risk his own life by flying with Air Commodore Mehar Singh. On May 24, 1948, Air Commodore Singh landed a Dakota aircraft on the highest airstrip in the world. Not taking any risk would have been the worst risk, but the courage of the two men even challenged death.

Major General Thimaya assured the people of Ladakh in Leh that the reinforcement would be flown within a day. But the promise could not be kept. No aircrafts were available, no troops could be spared and the weather was very challenging. Lt. Col. Prithi Chand sent a strongly worded message to the headquarters of Sri Division, "Had no promises been made and forgotten, morale would not have suffered so."

The President of the Buddhist Association of Ladakh also sent a message, alleging that the promises of immediate help would 'deceive' the people unless troops were sent by air very same day, all would be lost and 'no cries of distress will reach your ears from tomorrow.'

The headquarters of Sri Division said that it was only in May 31 and June 1 that a company of 2/4 Gorkha Rifles could land in Leh. The headquarters also said that a detachment of 2/8 Gorkha Rifles had left Manali on foot but it could reach Leh only by July; 1948. The town of Leh was poorly defended. It was a golden opportunity for the invaders to capture it. Through a new demarcated line, a buffer zone was expected by the enemy and Britishers over the Gilgit and Ladakh region. It was a completely demoralised attack even after the Instrument of Accession had been signed legally under balanced circumstances. Shadow help by British to Pakistani created a dark hole that Indian Armed Forces needed to go all hell alone with all available resources to retake the captured land and drive the enemies back behind the Radcliffe Line.

On 13 March, a public meeting was arranged by Lt. Col. Prithi Chand outside the British Residency building, known as Karzo Palace. At 1100 hours, people gathered outside the building. Lt. Col. Prithi Chand lowered down the British flag and hoisted the National flag of India. People celebrated the moment in a Buddhist tradition. The soldiers of X-Force displayed their weapon drills. The national anthem was sung by the people for the first time. People celebrated the moment by cheering 'Ki Ki So So Lhargyalo and 'Hindustan Zindabad'. The soldiers presented arms when the local band was played. The air was filled with the spirit of free will and patriotism. After the ceremony, Lt. Col. Prithi Chand addressed the people and assured them that the Indian Army had come to stop the invaders. He said, "We come to protect your 'chortens' (Ashes of your fathers) and the gompas. May the blessings of Lord Buddha rest on them." He also informed that Sonam Narboo, a foreign-trained engineer from Ladakh had started constructing the Leh airfield.

The airstrip became a ray of hope piercing the darkest clouds that soldiers and supplies would start coming in for the defence of Ladakh. Jammu and Kashmir suddenly turned into a core of war zone. The valleys of Kashmir and Ladakh took a drastic change under the building of reinforcement and troop mobilisation. Somewhere in Leh, a heart was thumping by seeing the massive military formation over the region that it continued towards the vast unprotected land of Nubra. The valley needed to be protected, if the region was not protected, all villages sitting on the lap of the Nubra region would be erased by the enemies.

A man in uniform asked for the volunteers to come forth and join hands with the regular soldiers to protect their motherland. When he asked the crowd to raise their hands if they would like to volunteer, a 17-year-old boy, who had passed his middle school examination in February 1948 laid aside his books and became the first volunteer to join the volunteer force. He was none other than Chhewang Rinchen. Many people had reluctance because of the in-born abhorrence of violence but soon after, many Nubrans volunteered to join Rinchen to save their motherland. The urge in him to protect the land where he was born and grew extended his valour to be a soldier.

25th March 1948, was a red-letter day in the career of Chhewang Rinchen as he was taken to Subedar Bhim Chand of 2 Dogra for basic weapon training. When he reached the training area, he was asked by Subedar Bhim Chand that why he wanted to join the volunteer force. In reply, Rinchen said, "It was just God's will and Lord Buddha's mercy over my country." Through this epic reply, he gained the confidence of Lt. Col. Prithi Chand and Subedar Bhim Chand. Still, a tension was roaming in the mind of Subedar Bhim Chand that how a 17-year-old boy would stand in front of a troop of thousand soldiers, what he would do if he started running out of ammunition, how he would counter the brutal bayonet charges and grenade attacks without knowing the future of Chhewang.

Subedar Bhim Chand did not doubt his courage but the war front was different. Rinchen saw the tension in his instructor's face. He admitted that he had to face a lot of difficulties but just because of his comfort and safety, he couldn't let his motherland being invaded by the enemy. Chhewang Rinchen, the Kalon of Leh, and some Dogra soldiers of the State Forces who had seen long years of service in the Army appreciated Rinchen's ambitions and capabilities.

During the training period, Rinchen was given some negative scenarios:

"Do you know what would happen to you if grenade bursts close to you?"

"Suppose an LMG/MMG is fired on your bunker and it collapses killing all the occupants?"

"What would happen to you if an enemy soldier made a bayonet charge on you and the bayonet penetrated through your abdomen and your intestine gushed forth?"

Nothing discouraged and deterred Rinchen. He never answered back. He kept himself quiet but focused more on his training. Those negative scenarios only made him determined than ever, more steadfast, more resolute, and more dedicated to the mission of protecting his motherland.

Ten days of crucial training made Rinchen competent in the elementary art of war, despite his age and immaturity. The soft skin on his palm hardened by the weapons. He also gained plenty of confidence to lead his men against the invaders. Subedar Bhim Chand became convinced that Rinchen had made a grade. Rinchen was provided with a sten gun and some ammunition. Green signal was given to him to recruit volunteers from Nubra Valley to face the invaders. Not even without a second's delay, he moved to Nubra from Leh to raise a local Nubran Volunteer Force with the help of Stanzin Tsering, and the Headman of the village Tegar.

When Rinchen came back to his village, he requested the villagers to gather on the ground. He then proceeded to explain the situation to the people and requested them to send at least one family member to join him to fight the enemy. He proved that a leader could not just command but also convince his people to initiate for a noble cause. No parents would agree to let their sons and nephews join the volunteer force. They thought Rinchen was a madcap, just gone crazy, and mentally challenged. The villagers said:

"Who would send his son to the front with you to be butchered?"

"They will all just become gun-fodder for the enemy's bullets."

"They will just make minced meat out of all of you and throw it in front of their dogs."

"Do you know-how you would be tortured if you were caught and made a prisoner of war?"

These questions did not make Rinchen feel discouraged. He did not lose his cool and very politely asked the seniors of the village, "But what is the alternative in your mind?"

The villagers had no answer to give for the reasonable question he raised. They just shrugged their shoulders and felt nonplussed. After a pause some villagers said:

"Let us depend on the mercy of Lord Buddha."

"It is not our job; why should we bother about it? It is the responsibility of the Government to do something."

"We are peace-loving people; we abhor war. War brings nothing but ruin and destruction."

"And why should anyone attack us? Ladakh has not known war for ages."

Rinchen tried hard to convince the villagers that it was the people who form the Government and became the shield of the land. "If you do not come forward to help the Government in the times of distress, the country will be raided by the enemy. Gompas will be desecrated, idols of Lord Buddha will be destroyed, chastity of our womenfolk will be violated, and our houses will be looted and burnt. Are you prepared for this?"

His words brought the spark. He considered himself fortunate, he did not know that he was a leader who could even give optimism even to a most pessimistic person. His cool mind, calculated and logical arguments did not make any dents on the minds of his seniors. They agreed to send their sons and nephews with Rinchen to defend their motherland. After a pause, Rinchen extended gratitude to his father and uncle who supported his stand.

Around three hundred Nubrans and Ladakhis volunteered to join with Rinchen. They followed Rinchen blindly for a common cause that it was to defend the sacred motherland. With the young volunteers, Rinchen rushed towards Leh to get the basic weapon and military training. They got their weapon training under Subedar Bhim Chand. Lt. Col. Prithi Chand imparted training to the volunteers. Rinchen was given the command of the volunteers. Rinchen named the troop the 'Nubra Volunteer Force', later it was renamed as the 'Nubra Guards'.

With just thirteen days of training, the troop was ready to be deployed. Lt. Col. Prithi Chand told Richen to deploy, with his troop, on the right bank of the river Shyok. Rinchen and his men started marching towards Shyok River. After ten days of day-night march by foot, they reached the river Shyok and crossed it. The same day they crossed Utmaru Waris mountain peak and reached Chumik La. There they saw a Pakistani post and observed its strength and movement. On June 10, 1948, Rinchen and his men launched a surprise attack. The enemy had no reply for the attack but to retreat. They fled, leaving behind two dead men with three rifles and some ammunition. This was an auspicious beginning to the career of Rinchen. After capturing Chumik La, Rinchen and his men moved towards Dzongpolas. They silently observed the movements, launched a surprise attack, and captured the post. By capturing Dzongpolas, the enemy was pushed back to Baidangdo.

After a few days, Subedar Bhim Chand reached Dzongpolas. He was elated by Rinchen's deeds and praised him. The position at Dzongpolas was strongly held by Rinchen and his men. Subedar Bhim Chand then sent Rinchen on patrol duty with a platoon. The platoon was known as Deskit Platoon. They had hardly moved some distance when they saw some Pakistani unarmed invaders. On seeing Rinchen and his platoon, the Pakistani invaders started running but Rinchen ordered his men to chase them. He intended to make them prisoners. His men had hardly turned a knoll in their pursuit when an ambush was launched from a post that was hidden from their sight. Rinchen along with his platoon took shelter behind a boulder.

When the enemy started firing towards the boulder, it began to disintegrate and a bullet whizzed past Rinchen's woollen worsted cap but luckily his head remained safe under the cap. Rinchen observed the enemy position and ordered his men to open fire in that direction. In the exchange of fire, one of the brave guardsmen, Chultim, was killed. Rinchen already lost one of his men and was running out of ammunition. With heaviness in his heart, he decided to retreat and started moving towards his post at Dzongpolas.

A few days later, Lt. Col. Prithi Chand received a message in Leh that the troop of 2/4 Gorkha Rifles which had been detailed to check the invaders in the Indus Valley had been ambushed by the enemy in Domkher on 26 June. They were attacked by nearly 600 invaders. After the ambush, the invaders reached Taru. Now Leh was just 16 kilometres away. A threat on the Leh airfield was palpable. The troop of 2/8 Gorkha Rifles, which arrived to Leh on 5 July via Manali route, was sent to reinforce the troop of 2/4 Gorkha Rifles. But both troops retreated soon as they faced heavy casualties. Major Hari Chand, who was commanding the Gorkha troops was missing for a while and was feared to be killed in action till he returned safely to Leh.

In the last week of June 1948, about 150 men of the Nubra Guards were deployed to protect Leh with just 20 regular soldiers.

Nearly 150 Nubra Guards were still fighting against the invaders in the Shyok valley under Subedar Bhim Chand and Rinchen. The Garrison in Leh issued orders to all Indian and State Forces to converge and rush towards Leh for its defence. An order was also issued that the Nubra Guards should be disbanded and all arms and ammunition issued to them should be withdrawn immediately.

The order of disbanding the Nubra Guards would have left the Nubra Valley completely unprotected. The news created great panic among the people of Nubra Valley. People started leaving their homes to find safety in Leh that became unbearable for Rinchen to witness his homeland being offered as a gift to the invaders. He asked for advice and guidance from his elders in the neighbouring area, such as Maulavi Ghato Ali of Partapur village, Rigzin Namgial, the Lonpo of Hundar, Stanzin Tsering, the Headman of the village Tegar, and Lama Sondus. They listened to Rinchen and advised him that he should continue to make determined efforts to raise a new volunteer force for the defence of Nubra Valley. They also assured him to provide him with all assistance in this patriotic cause.

Fortified by their assurances and with a burning desire to fight for the protection of his homeland, he went to the family temple and bowed his head before Lord Buddha and other Gods and Goddesses to seek their blessings for fulfilling the task which he had taken. In July, Rinchen crossed Khardung La (5,602 metres) by foot along with Stanzin Tsering to reach Leh. Rinchen placed his case review before Lt. Col. Prithi Chand at Zorawar Fort in Leh by requesting to reequip the Nubra Guards for the protection of Nubra Valley. Then Lt. Col. Prithi Chand invited Chhewang Rigzin, the Kalon of Leh for consultation.

Lt. Col. Prithi Chand had admired young Rinchen for his courage, determination, and spirit of loyalty for his motherland. But at that time, he also had some misgivings.

"What if Nubra Guards were defeated and taken captive or they surrendered on their own and their arms and ammunition fell into the hands of the enemy?"

Lt. Col. Prithi Chand was perhaps in two minds. "To give weapons to Rinchen's Nubra Guards and run the risk of losing them to the enemy or not to give them any weapons and thereby run the risk of seeing the Nubra Valley being overrun by the Pakistani invaders," he failed to decide. Finally, Rinchen came forth with the assurance, "No, Sir, there is no question of surrendering myself or my weapons to the enemy. My fighting spirit shall never die." Chhewang Rigzin, the Kalon of Leh became the guarantor for young Rinchen and gave him full support.

Lt. Col. Prithi Chand spoke to his higher officials to revive the Nubra Guards. After a discussion, Lt. Col. Prithi Chand got the green signal from them. Then he issued the arms and ammunition to Rinchen and his men. With the given stock of arms and ammunition, Rinchen rushed towards Nubra Valley to take up the job in his hands. On the way to Nubra, he met caravans of people who left Nubra to find shelter in Leh. He then requested people to go back to their homes and made up their minds to assist him in doing something to drive away the invaders. Most of them agreed to return their homes and extend helping hands to the Nubra Guards. On the way, Rinchen gave basic training to Stanzin Tsering in handling a rifle- its loading, aiming, trigger operation, and firing some rounds on the target. Rinchen then enlisted Stanzin Tsering in the Nubra Guards as his second-in-command.

Skardu fell into the hands of the enemy on 14 August 1948. The invaders were moving towards Leh. After reaching Leh, Rinchen recalled all the Nubra Guards to join him. With his ill-equipped force, Rinchen left for Skuru, the Gate of Nubra. When he had arrived at Skampuk, Rinchen received a piece of news that the Pakistani invaders had become very aggressive and sent an open demand to Partapur village to provide them 200 riding ponies, 100 loading ponies, and 300 porters as support to the invaders marching to Leh via Khardung La. Rinchen assumed that the invaders were planning to cross the Shyok River by Zhaks (improvised rafts made with animal skins) close to Skampuk. Rinchen decided to ambush when they would cross the river.

One fine morning, the invaders reached the other side of the Shyok River. A section of the enemy forces boarded a few zhaks to cross the river. Rinchen and his men were already in position and they were well hidden behind some boulders. Rinchen instructed his men not to fire a single bullet until the first zhak touched the bank so that they could capture the invaders alive. But one Nubra Guard fired a bullet when one of the zhaks reached mid-stream. Their ambush failed, so other Nubra Guards also started firing.

They killed a few invaders while the rest of them jumped into the river and swam back. The invaders on the other side of the river also started firing but due to the surprise attack, they got panicky and retreated towards Hundri village.

Leaving a few men to hold the position strongly, Rinchen advanced with his men to Skuru Nullah intending to put up a strong defence. The civilian population of Skuru village was shifted to Terchey village. However, all young men in the village volunteered to join Rinchen with whatever weapon they could lay their hands on. Rinchen then destroyed the Skuru Nullah Bridge to slow down the enemy movement. He thought from his enemies point and took decisions accordingly; his judgements and assumptions offered advantages to the Nubra Guards.

Within a week, many people from the valley joined the Nubra Guards. They came with swords, spears, and muzzle-loading guns. They also brought supplies such as sattu, meat, flour, apricots, and chang (local beer). The driving force behind all the activity to mobilise the Nubrans for the defence of the valley included Rinchen's father, Kunzang Dorje, Rigzin Namgial Lonpo, and Chhewang Rigzin, the Kalon of Leh. The Nubra Guards was thus raised to approx. 300 men. One could say that the entire Nubra Valley had risen as one force. The root which held the Nubra guard was Rinchen.

The Pakistani invaders misjudged and mistook the Nubra Guards as regular jawans of the Indian Army. As a result, the invaders did not dare to attack the positions held by Nubra Guards for a few days. After about 8 days of waiting, on the dawn of the ninth day, the invaders attacked the Nubra Guards position with a company. The invaders had LMGs and 2" mortars. The Nubra Guards repelled the attack with heavy casualties in the enemy's side, while one of the Nubra Guards was killed in action. After facing such heavy casualties, the enemy abandoned the idea of crossing the river Shyok. They started building their defensive positions on the other side of the river but continued firing on the Indian positions.

The Headquarters of the Nubra Guards was situated in the Gompa. It was built on the top of a hill to overlook all the movements happening in the Nullah. The Pakistani invaders used their mortars to destroy the headquarters but fortunately, most of the mortar shells proved to be ineffective.

Chhewang Rinchen had only twenty-eight trained Nubra Guards with him but he asserted that not less than a company was deployed there to mislead the enemy. Rinchen divided his men into two teams. One team led by Rinchen carried out raids from different points and directions while another team started burning fires at different places to create a sense of extensive deployment of the forces. His plans succeeded well and the invaders were so disheartened that they never tried for open clashes and kept away. After a week, the invaders launched another attack in the midnight using hand grenades. The attack resulted in a few casualties in the Indian side. However, Rinchen's men continued to guard the post and repulsed the attack. Rinchen utilised the minimum resources but maximised the disguise to be treat to the invaders. His common sense and decision making became a key factor in the field.

One day, Rinchen received a letter from his father, Kunznag Dorje, in which he had given a message which was communicated to him by Hasan Mistri of village Baidangdo. Hasan Mistri and Rinchen's father were alter-egos and both were trade partners. Hasan Mistri was pro-India. He had sent his messenger especially across the border to pass on a special message: "Pakistani troops are expecting reinforcements and they are planning to kill or capture Kunzang Dorje's son who is the Commander of the Nubra Guards." In his letter, Hasan Mistri had advised Kunzang Dorje to warn his son Rinchen to be cautious and alert during his movements in the front.

The news was a message for Rinchen. It failed to threaten him, rather he decoded the message as a plan of invasion. He immediately wrote a letter to Rigzin Kalon, son of Chhewang Rigzin, the Kalon of Leh, beseeching him to talk with Lt. Col. Prithi Chand on his behalf and request Lt. Col. Prithi Chand to send reinforcements as soon as possible. Besides, Rinchen also sent a runner to Leh requesting Lt. Col. Prithi Chand for immediate reinforcement. The news that Rinchen and his men successfully defended Skuru and blocked the advance of the Pakistani invaders towards Leh had reached Lt. Col. Prithi Chand with the runner. Lt. Col. Prithi Chand sent a letter of appreciation and commendation along with a promise of immediate reinforcement in the form of a Company of the Gorkha Regiment and a detachment of J&K Militia (Ladakhis) and Artillery sections – one equipped with 3" mortars and another with an MMG.

The English translation of Lt. Col. Prithi Chand's letter which was in Urdu reads thus:

"My dear brave Chhewang Rinchen, Commander, Nubra Guards,

I have received a letter from Shri Rigzin Namgial in which he has written about the brave deeds performed by you and your guards. I am pleased to learn that all of you are facing the enemy with great bravery and courage. I am sending through this messenger some cartridges and hand grenades.

Here also our troops are facing the enemy with boundless valour and devotion.

In the Taru Front, many jawans were killed in action but succeeded in capturing the enemy post. The enemy also suffered heavy losses both in the life of their jawans and armament. Many were wounded as well. Our morale is high.

We have received some reinforcements – both arms and armament and troops also. By the Manali route also, one battalion has arrived. I will personally come with a Gorkha Company and a 3" mortar section, a medium machine gun and some other arms.

Also, one platoon of the newly raised 7 J&K Militia will be sent to you soon to reinforce your troops.

Till then I pray Lord Buddha to help you. Convey my Shabash to your men. Heartiest congratulations and good luck.

Jai Bharat

– Lt. Colonel Thakur Prithi Chand"

With this letter, Young Rinchen enamoured with support and strength of his people and Indian Army into this war, through this a cub was rising into being the Tiger of Nubra.

❑

Chapter 4

Blooming of a Warrior

Struggles never exhausted him. His tenacity was infinite. He was stoic, his suppleness on the field sources cleared the paths for him to defeat the circumstances that were hostile to India. It is correctly quoted that days of despair would mould the will of a soldier. His strongest armour was from the toughest scars. When Chhewang Rinchen was upholding the defence on the front with his guards fiercely, the warrior in him was grooming himself.

It was 20 August 1948, Lt. Col. Prithi Chand visited the front where Chhewang Rinchen was facing the adversary. The Lt. Col. was accompanied by Rinchen's father and his younger brother, Phuntsog Namgial. The heavy firing on the front kept Lt. Col. Prithi Chand and Kunzang Dorje at the village of Terchey. Lt. Col. Prithi Chand sent Rinchen's younger brother, Phuntsog to the front to deliver his message to Rinchen. Phuntsog was a 15-year-old boy who was curious to see the deployment of troops. When Phuntsog reached the front, Rinchen asked his Quarter Master Angdan to show his brother the deployment of the troops, both Pakistani as well as the Nubra Guards. Richen also warned them to be careful with their movements. However, God had a different plan that changed the course of deeds and destiny of Rinchen.

While returning, they were crawling through the trenches when somehow spotted by the enemy who immediately opened fire. Angdan was hit on his head. Phuntsog rushed to inform Rinchen but Angdan had been already shot dead. After a few minutes, a runner from another post reported that a guardsman was also killed by enemy fire. Rinchen lost two of his brave men in a single day. The loss of the two brave souls fuelled Rinchen's determination to defend the frontier with ancillary strategies. Seeing his men holding off the enemy under such hellish conditions propelled Rinchen to be lithe with his plans on unconventional strategies. Everything aside, being a bearer of the code of soldier, Rinchen tried his best to give his two fallen men a burial with full military honours that what he had seen during his school days happened on his palm too.

After the rituals of the funeral, Rinchen hurried towards the village Terchey in absolute determination to meet his father and Lt. Col. Prithi Chand. Lt. Col. Prithi Chand deployed a company of 2/8 Gorkha Rifles and a platoon of newly raised 7 J&K Militia (Ladakhi) under the command of Major Mathur as Rinchen and his men needed some rest after extensive fighting for almost two months. Rinchen was ordered to take Subedar Ishar Singh of 7 J&K Militia and other JCOs of 2/8 GR to Skuru defence posts and give them an idea of deployment of forces on either side and to report back by the first light of August 24 at Terchey to proceed to Deskit.

Soon after reaching Deskit, Rinchen was recruited to the 7 J&K Militia in appreciation of the services rendered by him and his men. Rinchen was initially recommended for being commissioned in the Indian Army but the order was later withdrawn because he was a non-matric, yet nothing stopped him from opening pages of the historic defence in the first Indo-Pak war. He was, however, given the Junior Commissioned rank of Jemadar (Equivalent to Naib Subedar) in August 25, 1948. It was August 25th, the day became significant in the career of Chhewang Rinchen. A reception was held to honour him in Deskit, the headquarters of Nubra Guards.

Lt. Col. Prithi Chand, addressing the locals, praised Rinchen for his bravery and appointed him to be a part of 7 J&K Militia. Rinchen was not issued any uniform. He was given, on loan, a uniform belonging to a JCO of 2/8 GR. He is a soldier who executed his duties on a heroic scale even before donning the uniform and etching the rank and title of Indian Army on his chest. Rinchen was known for his untainted spirit to serve the nation at such a young age. Never had a person been recruited directly as Jemadar in the Indian Army and certainly not at that young age. Rinchen was only seventeen plus when his escapades are umpteen.

In the history of Indian Army, Rinchen was the youngest and bravest JCO who, for all practical purposes, was 'untrained' in the art of warfare. Like there is an unwritten rule of natural order that a tiger does not need to be trained to go for hunting, for sure the dazzling heir of Stakre lineage, Rinchen had natural acceptance for the military role. No matter how peaceful and composed his childhood was in Sumur, destiny had different plans for him. A curious child from Sumur made his purpose to serve in the military at the behest of the transformation he had in Leh during his teenagehood. Nevertheless, this nation at its forge also saw the rise of such dazzling stars in the north who paved the way for the art of mountain warfare with the code of the Indian Army. This was the first phase of Rinchen's legacy which he proceeded to scribble on the soil of our nation. His sane deeds were palpable on that day against the Gilgit frontier facing the Pakistani forces. A young warrior commenced his journey to magnify the defence of our nation.

During September 1948, Lt. Col. Prithi Chand formed a local government to function under the Colonel H.S. Parab, who had arrived to Leh at the end of August to take the charge of Military Governor of Ladakh. Rinchen's leave had ended and he happened to be with Lt. Col. Prithi Chand. In Leh, Rinchen was assigned to the task of raising a company of Nubra Guards and selecting 50 of them to operate as guerrilla force under him. It was a pioneering moment for him, as it was known in the lap of the Himalayas, not even the Britishers were able to effectively operate in the highest altitudes. Only the child of the mountain knew the best—bitterness of the cold air rushing into the lungs of his men. The mountain peaks were his playgrounds that Rinchen knew each fold and valley of the terrain. The upfront raising of the guerilla unit built a tiny but diamond-like hard defence for northern command during the war.

The locally raised boys knew the region well around Ldumbra in Western Ladakh and it was them whom Rinchen could count on when survival in the merciless atmosphere was the prime task. They were standing in with available resources they had from the Army. The unit was ready to serve the nation before carrying the mark of the Indian Army, maybe that was one of the moments in the unification of our nation by a spirit that the world never noticed.

Rinchen selected his men in a specific order according to their superior instincts of operating in high ranges, also those who could climb high mountains where there were no tracks, who could sleep in the snow even in the extreme cold weather, who could march like a commando and who could be alive to fight in the harsh conditions with little food and water. No war ever took place on the earth which was merciful to the men who fought, sometimes it was the mother nature who became the first line of the enemy. She was harsh on both the sides, but Rinchen's selected guards knew till the toe how to fight and survive with ease. Rinchen personally trained the men to use LMGs, mortars, and all types of grenades with the help of Gorkha troops. On the completion of the training, Rinchen took over the command of the guerrilla force. He was assigned various tasks to raid and capture several posts held by Pakistani invaders.

The first important task assigned to Rinchen was to capture the Lama House which was held by the Pakistani invaders on the other side of river Shyok near Hundori. It was at a height of approx 4,500 metres. Rinchen led the mission with a small detachment of his guerrilla force. The task was extremely hazardous and involved an arduous march lasting several days during inclement weather and along treacherous routes. From Skuru, he proceeded to Deskit and then marching along the river Shyok, he reached Kubet Bridge. Crossing the bridge at night, Nullah Chakri Chubab was the destination where he established his base.

The next morning, he ordered manpack bases and reached the altitude of 4,500 metres by the evening. The next day, he along with his men started climbing and reached the height of approx 5,000 metres at about 1130 hours. From there, they could easily see the Pakistani post. After lunch, Rinchen left on a recce to check the Pakistani post with his guide Zamkhan Chhewang, and Havildar Tashi Motup. After removing their long gonchas, they crawled down the slope like an ibex. They were approximately 350 metres away from the Pakistani post. Observing through binoculars, Rinchen saw that the post was held by a platoon, and around 25 men were engaged in the construction of a wall around that post. It was very difficult for Rinchen and his men to approach the Pakistani held post since the elevation of the posts and natural hurdles around the place was a problematic situation for them. What could stop the soldiers who were full of with spirit?

After returning from recce, Rinchen briefed his men about the attack. He divided his men into three sections. One section was to support cover from the right flank, the second was the centre, and the third was led by Rinchen himself to launch the attack from the left. The attack was planned to be launched during night. The ground was covered with snow and it was slippery. Amid the darkest, Rinchen's men had to find their way with the help of ropes, they were into the blind warfare-maze. Every sense of the body took the role of eyes by sensing the minuscule things during the climb with absolute silence. They could reach the enemy post only at about 0300 hours. After the sections had taken up their positions, Rinchen, along with Zamkhan Chhewang by his side and the section behind him, launched the attack.

As they reached close to the bunker, the sentry posted there sighted them and opened fire. Taking cover from the fire, Rinchen threw a grenade and made a bayonet charge on the main bunker before the post got alerted. A major portion of the enemy deployed was destroyed and the remaining ran pell-mell in their undergarments to save their lives. Amongst the dead was their Platoon Commander, Sergeant Major Mota Hasan of Gilgit Scouts, weighing about 250 pounds so appropriate to his name. As Rinchen's men reached the Lama House, they found it completely deserted. The enemy forces had run away without offering resistance. Rinchen captured one sten gun and thirteen rifles. His position in the Lama House was later reinforced by a Platoon of 2/4 GR, with a section of 3" mortar commanded by Subedar Moti Lal Gurung.

After the battle in the Lama House, news arrived that Skuru position was recaptured by the Pakistani invaders causing heavy casualties in the Indian side and capturing a section of 2/8 GR with arms and ammunition. The fall also meant the descent of Terchey village close by all the surrounding hills of Skampuk. Thus, giving the enemy total control of that area. The Indian troops fell back to Skampuk village hill position approximately fifteen kilometres behind. After the fall of Skuru, the command of the Nubra Sector was taken over by Major S.J.S Bhonsle, the 2IC of 7 J&K Militia. Once again, the troops succeeded in slowing down the enemy's advance and recapturing some of the hill features including the post on top of the Skamppuk Hills. Subedar Nar Bahadur whose platoon achieved success on the front was awarded Vir Chakra later.

In the meantime, Colonel H.S. Parab arrived for a visit. He instantly ordered an attack on the Terchey Pak positions after assessing the tactical situation in the Nubra Valley. The code name given to the operation was 'Operation Chang'. Almost three hundred volunteers armed with swords, axes, spears, and muzzle-loaded guns were enrolled for the purpose of attack. No men expected deadly weapons as they themselves were the most dangerous with their hearts full of patriotism. Rinchen formed a rear of the attacking force along with some Gorkha troops of 2/8 GR supported by a section of 3" mortar and a section of MMG.

The action plan included free servings of Chang and Arak to the volunteers and to the rest of the personnel. Then they mounted the ponies to reach after the first light. The forces attacked the enemy's defence positions under the effect of the drink but there was no drawback. But they had no idea about their position. As a result, they faced reverses, resulting in total confusion and failure of Operation Chang. The remaining troops and volunteers, beaten and disorganised, withdraw to the Skampuk position.

After the failure of Operation Chang, Colonel Parab called Rinchen for an interview at the Tactical Headquarters at Hundar village. Rinchen presented himself before Colonel Parab in his uniform which was nothing but his clothes, a long goncha, worsted cap, and pabo shoes, with a Sten gun under his arm and two hand grenades tied with his skark (belt). Colonel Parab asked Rinchen," Are you the young guy who has been fighting so badly against the Pakistani invaders?" Rinchen gave a reply that Col. Parab praised Rinchen for his courage, boldness, and determination. Col. Parab asked him to go and bring the MMG, fired from a Pak defensive position at a point below the Lama House, as a memento of his victory.

The same night, Rinchen along with his three volunteers, each equipped with a personal arm and two hand grenades, left for the mission. Their plan of attack was to get as close as possible to the Pak position and throw hand grenades into their gun positions before they became aware of the attack. When Rinchen and his men were crawling towards the Pak position, a stone on the slope got dislodged with the result that the sentry got alerted and raised the alarm, "Dushman! Dushman!"

In the puzzled moment, Rinchen threw a hand grenade into the Pak post rather aimlessly and ran for cover. The enemy opened fire with the MMG and threw a few grenades as well. Though Rinchen did not suffer any casualties, he failed to fulfil the mission. Every incident became his lessons. He learned the value of time and decision making. He realised the fact that excuses would never be accepted when one left his home behind and decided to stand in the frontiers.

One day, Major J.S. Sidhu, the Sector Commander, sent a message ordering Rinchen to send his pony for his use. It was Rinchen's favourite pony and was very close to his heart, so he refused. Rinchen was called to the Sector HQ, Hundar, where Major Sidhu used strong language, "Tumney kya isse Khalaji da ghar samjha; hum tumko naukri se dismiss Kar dega." This hurt the ego of Rinchen. He replied in equally strong language, "Mujhe dismiss toh kariye." Rinchen threw his Sten gun in front of Major Sidhu and returned home knowing well that it could be the end of his military career. But the next day, he received a summon from Colonel Parab. When Rinchen reached Leh, he had gone to see his Commanding Officer, Lt. Col. Prithi Chand and told him about the unfortunate incident that had happened between him and Major Sidhu. Lt. Col. Prithi Chand knew well how useful Rinchen was at the critical juncture. He ordered Rinchen to take charge of a Platoon of 7 J&K Militia and proceed to the Taru front. Noticing Rinchen's dress, he ordered the Quarter Master to issue him a proper uniform.

After a couple of days, Rinchen was ordered to return to the Nubra Sector and take over the command of the Nubra Guards and the guerrilla troops. Soon after reaching Nubra, Rinchen reported to Major Sidhu and apologised for what happened between them in the past. The unsavoury incident was forgotten. In the best traditions of the Indian Army, Major Sidhu and Chhewang Rinchen shook hands as fine soldiers and toasted a drink. Rinchen felt condoned and relaxed for a while but the war didn't end here yet. The moment was yet to arrive which would be considered a catapult in stopping the enemy invasion and save the territory of Jammu and Kashmir.

By November 1948, the Indian Army had captured Zojila pass and was advancing in the Kargil Sector. The incident unnerved the Pakistani invaders in the Nubra Sector and they started withdrawing their troops. Reports were received by Indian forces from the local people of Hundari and Terchey. Major Sidhu, the Sector Commander, decided to give a hot pursuit to the enemy forces while they were withdrawing. The Indian forces soon occupied Changmar, Chumik La, and Baigdangdo. As the Indian troops reached Dzongpolas, Hasan Mistry, the Headman of Baigdangdo came out to meet them carrying a white flag and assured full support from the village for the Indian Army.

As the Indian Army entered Baigdangdo, they were welcomed by the local male population but the women and children were conspicuous by their absence. They had run away to hide in the Nullah, fearing that the Indian troops might also behave like the Pakistani invaders who had committed brutal atrocities. Rinchen was detailed by the Sector Commander to convey the women and children hiding in Nullah with the good intentions of the Indian forces and persuade them to return to their homes. As Rinchen went to Nullah accompanied by a section of the Gorkhas, the women and children, on seeing them coming towards them, got frightened and started withdrawing into the adjoining hills. Rinchen explained them in their language that the Indian forces had come to protect their honour from the Pakistani invaders and they would be treated like their mothers and sisters. It took great efforts that Rinchen succeeded in bringing them back to their homes. Their faces were covered with black pigment, only their eyes and teeth being visible. Rinchen advised them to wash their faces and assured them that no one from India would ever misbehave with them. Next day, they appeared with their faces clean. Marching on the village was quite another thing but more it was struggling to keep India unified with its crown as we know today the entirety of Jammu Kashmir. Every word of Rinchen blooded with honesty and honour of his nation and finally, it made a difference and turned every living soul of the village into supportive pillars to the Army.

The advance of the Indian forces was halted at Baigdangdo on November 6 as the enemy had built a strong defensive position on the Black Rock. It was further strengthened at Takkar Hill and Tebedu Hill and Nullah, respectively on the left and right flanks. The tide had, however, begun to turn against Pakistan. In the Nubra Valley, as elsewhere, December 1948 proved to be a bad month for them when they were dislodged from several strategically important hill features.

In December 15, 1948, Rinchen was ordered to capture Takkar Hill with the help of his guerrilla forces while the main force was ordered to attack the Black Rock feature. Both the operations were successful and resulted in heavy casualties on the enemy side. However, on being ousted from the positions, the enemy took up new positions in Chulunkha Nullah and continued to hold the Tebedo Hill and Nullah position; thus, halting the pursuit undertaken by the Indian forces.

On December 22, 1948, Rinchen was directed to capture Tebedo Hill and Nullah and the surrounding hill points that were in the occupation of the enemy. Supported by his guerrilla force and 20 young men from Baigdangdo engaged as porters, Rinchen left to accomplish the mission assigned to him.

It was the last week of December 1948. There had been heavy snowfall and it was extremely cold. They spent a night in the base of the high mountain. The next morning, Rinchen with a handful of selected volunteers started climbing the steep mountain slopes. Stanzin Tundup, Deskit, and Rinchen cleared the path for the rest of his men. By sunset, they reached the top of the hill which was at a height of approximately 6,400 metres and waited for the rest of his men to arrive. But they were nowhere to be seen. The small group of three 'musketeers' shared thick homemade bread, sattu, and a bottle of arak.

It was snow, snow, and snow all around. The entire Nubra Valley and its adjoining heights were brutal at night during winter. For a person living in a tropical region, it would be a freezing hell experience in such terrain, but it was a completely different aspect for the people who lived in the severe condition since birth. It was understood that the enemy had difficulty in operating in this harsh winter. Meanwhile, Rinchen and his guards had no other alternative but to dig into the snow and spend the whole night in the snowy cave, sleeping in the snow, with nothing underneath and nothing above. Despite the intense cold and high altitude, none of them suffered from frostbite. The next morning, they tried to observe the movements of the Pakistani position but nothing could be seen from that point. By 1100 hrs, the rest of his men joined them, and after having some sattu and tea, they started. It was afternoon, they reached a gap amid the mountains covered with snow. This was just above the enemy position, situated at a height of approximately 6,000 metres.

Neither Rinchen's men saw the Pakistani post, nor the Pakistani watched Rinchen's movements, so they decided to spend the night in the gap. They finalised the plans for the attack while having dinner with hot thukpa. One section under Rinchen was to make the assault, while another, under Chering Palges, was to give him support from the right. The third under Rigzin Phunchok was to cut off the enemy on the left flank. The next day, early morning, Rinchen's three sections started their mission and when they were approximately 350 metres away from the enemy, they found that a Nullah separated them from the target.

It was decided that the section under Chering Palges should offer cover, while Rinchen climbed up the ridge without being observed by the enemy. They were still approximately 100 metres away from the enemy post when the day dawned with bright sunshine. In the enemy post, while one section was engaged in sentry duty, about 25 men were enjoying smoking hukkah. Rinchen was carrying a 2” mortar while a coolie from Baigdangdo named Ali Sarpopa, was carrying the mortar shells. Targes Hundar was carrying an LMG. Rinchen took the LMG and fired the full magazine on the hukkah party killing about half a dozen of them. The rest of them ran pell-mell to seek cover in their bunkers. Rinchen started bombing their bunkers with 2” mortar shells. One of the bombs scored a hit on the bunker and many were killed. Others who came out into the open were killed one by one.

With supporting fire from the left by the section of Rigzin Phunchok and the support given by 2” and 3” mortars, MMGs were captured from the Black Rock and Rinchen pulverised the enemy positions. Rinchen then ordered a bayonet charge. On entering the post, his men captured wounded Pakistani soldiers. A search of the dead bodies in the post revealed how they had looted the local people.

While Rinchen was carrying out the mopping operation, the Indian men erroneously opened fire resulting in a coolie getting killed. Rinchen was miraculously saved. The entire party took cover immediately. When Rinchen found that the fire was mistakenly opened on them, he shouted ordering them to stop firing. When his shouting had been proved ineffective, he had to ask one of his men, who was in the Pakistani bunker to raise his monkey cap on the bayonet of his rifle to indicate that the firing was being directed on allies. This proved effective and finally, the firing stopped. After occupying the Tebedo post, Rinchen’s party went in hot pursuit of the retreating enemy, coming across many wounded and many died on the way.

Later, the Pakistani prisoners informed the Indian forces that the Pak Company HQ was located at Tebedo Nullah. This information pinpointed the core of enemy operations finally in the eyes of the Indian Army; blunt but hammering blow it would be for the enemy. It was not so simple as how it looked and without wasting a fraction of second, Rinchen's Party pushed forward and reached Nullah by midnight but found that it had been deserted proving the complexity of the scenario and lack of solid human intelligence. Rinchen and his men returned to the base. The occupation of the Tebedo post was celebrated through bada khana prepared with the large number of rations left behind by the Pakistani invaders during their hurried withdrawal. Chhewang Rinchen's Nubra Guards spent the day enjoying the bada khana and rum enabled the Pakistani invaders to withdraw safe to the Chulunkha complex and build strong defences halting any pursuit planned by the Indian troops.

January 1949, a ceasefire was ordered by the Government of India. It was to be effective at 2359 hours before midnight of January 1-2, 1949. "It came like a bombshell. Given less than a week, the invaders could have been thrown out of the entire Baltistan," Rinchen lamented. Given the time Nubra guards had, it was a fitting blow to them especially for Rinchen, the day when they realised what golden opportunity they missed. Rinchen always regretted why he and his Nubra Guards wasted a day enjoying bada khana instead of giving hot pursuit to the fleeing enemy. Every incident equipped the warrior in him. His brain recorded the cohesiveness of the acts to react flawlessly.

Once the ceasefire was declared, the Indian Sector Commander in the region was invited by the Commander of the Pakistani Sector to have lunch in their Headquarters at Chulunkha. Accepting the invitation, the Indian Sector Commander along with Chhewang Rinchen and a few of his men, went to Pakistani

Sector Headquarters. The time they spent there was in an atmosphere of mutual cordiality and bonhomie. The Pakistani Sector Commander presented each member of the Indian side badges and caps of the Gilgit Scouts and pairs of woollen socks.

The young tiger, who penned down the historic fidelity by his valour, pioneered for the mountain warfare during the first day of the independent Indian Army raised with the capable and strong unit in the region which later became the cradle of Ladakh scouts in the future. Rinchen's critical time turned him a hero of the nation and his village. But inside his heart, one day of celebration made him unhappy for a brief time, the ceasefire was no good news for a soldier who aimed to bring absolute and every inch of the land back which belonged to his nation. But it didn't result in a way how he and his men expected. In honest regards, not a single soldier of the Indian Army was happy with this intervention of the UN under the political clothing which they fabricated in the name of peace.

Pakistan owns a chunk of Jammu Kashmir under its control and even today the resolution of the UN was not followed by Pakistan. Where the ceasefire occurs, is now known as the Line of Control which stretches far to the tip of the Siachen glacier. A soldier always remains alert in peacetime as the history taught us the lesson that the ceasefire, with conviction, made us abandon a part of our territory to illegal occupation by the adversary. Amid the chaos of ceasefire, the Indian Army also got the youngest Mahavir Chakra Recipient. The Tiger roared that day with might and honour. Even today, his breath echoes in the valley with the same rage whenever the fences are cut down to infiltrate.

❑

Chapter 5

The Youngest Mahavir

The nectar of the fresh war had just been sipped, under the behest of high peaks of the Himalayas in the Northwestern frontier, by the Indian Army. The world had just entered its new calendar. The year 1949 brought a historic shift in India's geographical shape. The map of India was reshaped. Jammu Kashmir became the crown of the Indian Union geographically, somehow derailed in the first week of 1949. An untold mockery and brazenly flawed ceasefire were drawn in haste by the world's brand-new model, the "United Nations" without a fair consensus.

The big loaves of the geopolitical stage, like the US and UK, growled on the sudden spark of war and stopped India from taking what rightfully belonged to it. The Indian Army managed to stop the invasion and adrift enemies enough to push them back and retake crucial regions but it was not enough, a big chunk of Kashmir remained under the clutches and occupation of Pakistan illegally.

The ceasefire was drawn and both side armies made to cease mounting. The government of both countries agreed to a truce under the clove of some idea of long-term peace. The United Nations Security Council Resolution 47 was penned with hope that both sides would accept the plebiscite and agree on a peaceful relationship further. For the world, it looked like UNSC did praiseworthy work in mid of 1948 by enacting the ceasefire commission for Jammu Kashmir to implement the enabled resolution but it merely stopped both countries from strangling each other again in the future.

To say honestly, the clauses in the resolution were never agreed by the Pakistani government in first place despite agreeing officially the plebiscite. The Resolution recommended a three step process. In the first step, Pakistan was asked to withdraw all its nationals who entered Kashmir for the sake of fighting. In the second step, India was asked to progressively reduce its forces to the minimum level required for law and order. In the third step, India was asked to appoint a plebiscite administrator nominated by the United Nations who would conduct a free and impartial plebiscite. But as wisdom whispered to the deaf ears, Pakistan never initiated the first step. It was a clear mockery to the international forum but also the blatant apathy towards the referendum on which they agreed to abide by thoroughly.

On January 21, 1949, the ceasefire came into effect. In February, the UNSC commission arrived at the Indian subcontinent. It had done a final but elusive ceasefire. Also stamped it forever which was marked and stretched from Radcliffe line, going through Kashmir, and moving through the valley to far north till Baltistan. Later, it became one of the most dangerous borders across the world. Fate turned into a fiend this time. A deep struggle to free the entirety J&K from the enemy's clutches stopped in between. From a diplomatic perspective, it was a win-win situation for India but the soldiers on the ground felt the ache in their hearts, seeing a half-shattered commitment to bring J&K region rightfully into Indian Union. It made a stomp of agony on our warriors as the Instrument of Succession didn't allow India to become whole with her shining silver crown of the Himalayas.

The troops were called off after having a truce meeting with the Sector Commander of the Pakistani Army at Chulunkha. Chhewang Rinchen, who was promoted to Jemadar by the last phase of the battle in his Nubra Guards, attended the meet as a part of protocols with his sector commander and few men of Pakistani counterpart. He still felt anguish and disheartened about the one-day delay that he and his men used for celebration and little rest. It was his unbridled belief that he could have wiped out all enemies and cleaned Baltistan, thus bringing it into Indian administration, but perhaps fate turned out to be the real enemy that day.

The war was over and Jemadar Chhewang Rinchen left with his troops in Leh after the sectoral commander meeting and the hollow bonhomie gesture which none of the soldiers ever acknowledged. This was the start of a long-term rivalry and the moment was riding on thin hope of an impoverished time in which both nations just stepped in with their armies standing as spearhead pointing at each other.

In the middle of January 1949, Rinchen reached Leh with his entire troop of Nubra Guards. Lt. Col. Prithi Chand and Colonel H.S. Parab welcomed the troops home. Indeed, it was a detrimental feeling but soon it turned out to be absolved memoir for Rinchen. He took time to realise that he saved his home and it was a victory, He saved the crown of India. His valour was insurmountable and stallion-like strength made sure the enemy could not take a grain of soil of Nubra Valley and Ladakh.

It was no less than the defence of Hot Gates of Thermopylae by King Leonidas and his 300 men. India witnessed a very stiff and intense defence of the land against the overwhelming force of the enemy. He was stalwart as he felt the surge of the great gallant in him that day but in the life of a soldier, the moment of feeling intrepid was only when he was facing the enemy and defending his motherland for a noble cause. When the entire Leh was in a joyous and exhilarating feel, Rinchen was standing tribulated behind his delectating and delighted men. A little get-together in HQ involved all senior members including Stanzin Dorje Kaga, especially Rigzin Namgial Lonpo who was much impressed by Rinchen's operations against the enemy and discussed the same greatly with commanding officers present there.

The 17-year-old young lionheart, who was raised in the Nubra Guards in mere few days, trained them, led them to fight and successfully thwarted enemies much behind to secure the valley of flowers and gift it as a crown on the shining head of India, was standing silent in the camp during dawn when troops were having a little celebration and chit-chatting including both Nubra Guards and JK Militia with Lt. Col. P.N. Kaul and Major Bhonsle, and even the Kalon was also present in the celebration. Lt. Col. Prithi noticed Rinchen, he walked towards him in a fervent state. He stood beside him while the entire camp was in a vibrant atmosphere, the corner was silent.

"It's curious to see the man of an hour standing in solitude, Jemadar!", Lt. Col whispered.

Rinchen suddenly noticed Lt. Col. Prithi was there, stunned to see him without noise there.

"I was just seeing our boys, Saabji.", he replied.

"It seems something is bothering you, son.", Lt. Col. pushed the concern he had.

"Can I ask you something, Saabji?" Rinchen swiftly said it.

"Go ahead soldier, ask.", Lt. Col. replied.

"Was it enough? Whatever we reclaimed? Should we be happy when the enemy themselves managed to take half of Kashmir from us?" Rinchen said. His heart was out in regret.

Seeing the unrelinquished and emboldened flame of unresolved quest in his eyes, Lt. Col. Prithi replied, "This is what makes us different from the civilians, son. See those cherished faces over there. Deep down they feel the same remorse as you but they are trying to be cheered up, do you know why?"

"Why Saabji?", Rinchen asked curiously.

"Because they saved their home and prevented more bloodshed of innocent villagers living in this valley. This war made us stand in unity and ushered us in an embarking stride to fight ahead to protect what we have now. We have something to stand for, we have our identity unified under one flag and one nation.", Lt. Col. said.

"But did we accomplish what we meant to?" Rinchen asked again in a slow tone.

"Enemy came with confidence that they will successfully invade all of J&K with Ladakh but failed to even cross the Baltistan; they are weeping for that after the ceasefire was declared. So, tell me is it not an optimistic accomplishment to defeat your enemy with their purpose?" Lt. Col. pushed his statement.

With a simple smile on his face Rinchen agreed "Ji Saabji, I think that's no more than victory."

The Lt. Col. Further emphasised, "Your concern is right in all ways but you already outdid many of your senior's expectations even though you are not a properly commissioned soldier. The entire nation is proud of you and your men".

"At ease soldier, relax now.", Lt. Col. walked away easing Rinchen with his words.

Rinchen took it as a wisdom and embraced whatever happened back there on frontiers but the regret remained with him all along till his last days. Somehow that alone pushed his potential further inflow in his service days. The entire day dissolved in the settling of the mind and souls of everyone after the war, significantly of Chhewang Rinchen.

The next day, soldiers of Nubra guards were talking about returning home in a few days. The wishes of troops reached Rinchen's ears and subsequently towards the HQ desk too. After a few days, in early March, the troops of Nubra Guards were allowed to go home for an ample period and were sent with the 7th Jammu Kashmir Militia under command of Lt. Col. P.N.Kaul with his second-in-Command officer Major S.J.S. Bhonsle. The Militia was attached to Jammu Kashmir Light Infantry as a new component of Northern Command after the war. This was then, the important structure of Northern Command and later tasked for securing borderline in eastern and western boundaries of Ladakh. Hailed as the children of mountains, Rinchen's newly raised guards became a cornerstone of the entire militia's standing. The men in Nubra Guards had such strong blood to survive in snowclad regions and were the ones who showcased their might in the devilish climate helping the 7th JK Militia to mount a successive attack on enemies.

It had been so many days since Rinchen had seen his mother and met her properly. When he heard his men wanted to go home, it suddenly created an urge in him to go home too. Four to five years had passed since he left home for Leh. In between this time, he visited only a few times to his birthplace and cradle of his inception of the journey. Rinchen sought permission from his superiors to go home with his men including his friend Tashi Motup whom he selected from Sumur village like others for Nubra Guards. Lt. Col. Prithi allowed them to go but ordered them to return within a month as they were crucial men for the newly raised unit and further needed for more military training and official commissioning into the forces. In a sense, JK Militia was paramilitary under the Ministry of Home Affairs. The guards went on to become a critical unit ahead under the leadership of Chhewang Rinchen following the Indo-Pak War in 1948.

When the march was in its last phase, Rinchen and his men left Leh to visit Sumur. The conscience of Rinchen munched the days back. It was a moment of great pride and paramount of change for him as he started to look at the valleys and all familiar sceneries started to hold his every memory back to the day. He stepped out of the village for the first time with Kalon. The time surely turned the tide of fate for him. A child with a calm and composed soul, with a desire to learn and help others turned himself into a soldier, 13-year-old Chhewang would not have believed that within four years what he would become. For someone, it could be as a transition of a village boy into a soldier who defended the valley and defeated the enemies. But deeply, it is a transcendence in which Rinchen himself believed when he first saw the parade and marching of troops in uniform.

As the dawn broke, all the boys reached the tiny hamlet and knocked at the doors of their home. Only the patient eyes of the parents could tell how thrilled they were to see their sons again. Being a soldier without adequate training was a hard job but what their families went through was nothing less than hardest. Going for an unexpected war was difficult but waiting for their return from the war was toughest for the families. Rinchen never changed alone, with him he transformed his village youngsters and his brothers. He showed them the path of great valour by the course of the future when the entire country took its first breath as united. Rinchen's mother plunged in tears when she had seen her son, how sparkling yet tearful was the moment that the flower that bloomed met its roots after ages. With love in all hearts, the Himalayan peaks also melted that evening. The functioning of India is in its own wheel today, after the early war with the neighbour who was born from India's own separated land, became possible through the courage of the families who have sent and will send their loved ones to protect the frontiers.

Rinchen's mother took her child into her arms and welcomed him while his father was seeing a soldier coming inside the home. Verily! both were right. She saw her son and he saw a soldier, the child of Kunzang Dorje and Jamyang Dolma was, then, a hero of the country.

It was a bright upright morning with calm wind across the valley, the sun was not warm but shining like a king over Sumur. Rinchen remembered his early days in the hilltops, river shores, bell sound of gompa, whistling air, horizon kissing the mountains and serene scenery of this little hamlet in the lap of Nubra.

Spring had arrived in the valley of flowers as the Nubra Guards returned home after the storm of war, but it was the first spring without the northwestern region of Karakoram ranges as a part of India. He took a deep and euphoric breath. He hushed into his returning memories as vividly his eyesight focusing on the view around the place he knew since his birth, unreal but a nostalgic trip he experienced when he walked into the village again like a child. But the villagers no longer saw him as a cheerful kid who grew up running in the small alleys and hills. They looked at the courageous man walking in front of them, who led the fight against invaders and defended the land of their birth. The reverence that he got from the villagers was unbelievable for him first. Humble by nature and faithful to his responsibilities, young Rinchen never expected much from anyone but he assuredly felt the warmth when people of Sumur came to see him in awe. Rinchen felt pure love in their respectful approach and villagers felt the radiance of the protector in him. Not just by him but by all the boys who were part of Nubra Guards and fought under the command of Rinchen.

Call it enlightening or realising of the moment but Rinchen felt the connection of his long time seeking. While witnessing a unique atmosphere, he understood that he had finally found his true purpose which he sought five years ago. His answer started its journey in Leh, led him in enemy frontiers to grow and finally ushered into the complete picture in the eyes of his people who were over the moon for being untouched by the enemy and felt safe after the war.

No wonder how cheerful he felt seeing his people in the village that day as his brothers in arms of the Nubra Guards also joined him. Together, they all walked around the village.

Looking at their appearance, anyone could say that they were just teenagers but knowing them, everyone recognised them as the heroes of Ladakh.

Three months later, spring arrived at its final month of the annual cycle in June. Leh was pleasant with its sweet cold but warm climate during daylight and chilly silent cold during the night. Rinchen and his boys had already returned to Leh and started their important segments of training in the camp with the 7 J&K Militia under the command of Lt. Col. P.N. Kaul and Major S.J.S Bhonsle. Both seniors of the Militia were discussing something while looking at Rinchen who was instructing his boys on the ground with basic training. Rinchen soon discovered that he was the subject of his senior's discussion. He got curious but kept his curiosity under his mind's blanket and continued his training with his units. Out of the blue, he noticed Major S.J.S Bhonsle appeared beside him, for a moment Jemadar Rinchen was startled seeing Major Saab there.

Rinchen took the step and saluted him.

Major Bhonsle hushed, "How's the training going on, Jemadar?"

"All good Saabji, they are grasping it well.", Rinchen replied in affirmation.

"Good to see, Jemadar!", Major assured.

"Any order for me, Saabji?", Rinchen asked.

"Not an order, but we have news for you." Major corrected.

"Ji Saabji, what is the news?" Rinchen asked humbly while standing in an attentive posture.

"A few months ago, when our defence administrative member Rigzin Namgial Lonpo told us about your war operations, we went on to check the sites personally to confirm. Jemadar, your efforts were brave and very crucial during the war, we are greatly impressed", Major Stated with a bold voice.

"I'm honoured Saabji, it was my duty.", Rinchen embraced the gratitude in a clean voice.

"If someone outdoes his duty and shows warrior-like effort towards his nation we call them Veer, Jemadar" Major added.

"Sorry, I didn't understand Saabji!", Rinchen puzzled.

"You proved your valour with quite mettlesome efforts, we are recommending your name for gallantry commendation, Jemadar Chhewang Rinchen! "Major consolidated his line.

Rinchen froze for a moment to grasp the entire news.

"I'm greatly honoured Saabji, thank you!" Rinchen responded.

"We are Proud of you, all the best.", Major ended the conversation and left the ground.

It was not the soldier's personality within him which echoed that day in his heavy sigh but his childhood self-sparked up listening to the news, who clamped his emotion and released his happiness. It took a moment for him to digest the news but Rinchen felt a surge of honour rush in his heart for the very first time like never before. He continued with his training with his brothers of the unit in the dazzling noon of the day. It was not the award which thrilled him but the recognition of a young boy. Not just for saying, but it is indeed authentic that 'Nothing can go unnoticed in Army'

Four days later, the auspicious Hemis festival came, one of the venerated and holy gompa in Leh was in the Hemis Monastery situated 45 km away from Leh. The Gompa was devoted to the 8th century Buddhist Guru Rinpoche (Padmasambhava), who was considered "Second Buddha" in the Drukpa Lineage of Tibetan Buddhist Culture. The festival was in the form of a dance performance to tribute the reincarnation of Buddha as Padmasambhava and it fell on the last month of spring around June according to Gregorian calendar. The whole of Leh including adjacent Monasteries in the region held this day as one of the sacred events at the end of spring. The vibe of celebration was continued even after the next day, the entire region dissolved into devotional euphoria, with jubilation and rejoicing the event in Tibetan traditional ceremonies. As the year pictured multiple emotions, the ecstasy in the wind was exotic.

The next day, soon after the festival, HQ received a humble invitation from Sankar Gompa for the sermons of His Holiness Kushak Bakula. All army officers, JCOs, official dignitaries and aristocratic elders of Leh like the Kalon of Ladakh were invited for the occasion of the sermon. Chhewang Rinchen was also invited for the sermon. It was an auspicious moment for him and he visited the gompa in the evening with his aides and seniors for the sermon. Many known faces were present in the hall but his eye caught an unknown pretty face across the hall sitting in front of him. His mind was puzzled about her, he felt like he saw her somewhere, but the memory was not giving enough push to realise who she was, she looked at Rinchen with a charming smile and turned herself towards the preparation of the sermon.

Rinchen was in the maze of identifying her face.

His Holiness Kushak Bakula started his sermon, all eyes were on him including her; She was dressed in ceremonial attire and was ardently focused on the sermon being delivered by His Holiness. It was quite straight forward that Chhewang Rinchen felt his heart was skipping a beat while seeing her. It was as if his soul made him overflow with curiosity to inquire about her. Words of the sermon by His Holiness might have taken the attention of the entire hall and the present invited attendees but Rinchen had struggled with his memory and his heart in accord with her. “Who is she? Did I see her somewhere? Why does this pretty person look familiar?” These were the barrage of questions hitting his mind all along. The sermon was over by then, He saw Kalon talking to the man who stood with the 15-year-old girl. Rinchen remained unfazed but he wanted to quench this curiosity. By the time it was obvious to him about her identity, his innocent heart concluded about liking her which he later realised. Rinchen, after a few moments found the Kalon alone, he gathered courage and asked him about the man and the girl with him. He clarified them and revealed that he was a family friend and the girl was the man's niece and coincidentally Rinchen knew her uncle Skalzang Rinchen Lonpo. Later, all dots were connected and finally Rinchen realised the entire narration about her and where he saw her for the first time.

It was during school days when Rinchen used to visit her house to call her father on behalf of Kalon for a drink every evening. He used to see a shy and quietly charismatic 10-year old girl in the house. She was Chuskit Dolma, and it had been five years since he saw her. She was a 15-year-old pretty girl when Rinchen's eyes stole her sight after years.

Chuskit Dolma belonged to one of the respected aristocratic families in Leh. Her father and uncle were well-known friends of Kalon. Chhewang Rinchen's heroism stories were whispered into the ears of some prominent figures of Chuskit Dolma's family. Eventually, she knew about him. Either it was fate or the hearts which brought them into the feeling of pureness that day in Gompa. Rinchen soon realised where his heart was heading. After the sermon, she left with her uncle. It turned out to be a special evening for him. Seeing her felt like he discovered his soul mate during the religious sermon, for him the evening was no less than a benediction from Lord Buddha.

Leh was a vast region but the populated settlement was enveloped in a small area, and her house was not much away from Kalon's residence. After getting a fresh projection of nostalgic moments five years ago, he got to know exactly where she lived. The days were calling out to him. It was certain Rinchen felt head over heels for her. Her little innocent glimpse whenever flickered in his mind, it used to give him a blushing smile; a pure love sparked somewhere in his heart for her.

He finally decided to go and talk to her.

After a couple of weeks, one day around the weekend he took off early from the camp and went to see her. It was early morning as he reached her residence. But he was reluctant to go inside the house. In a jiffy, he saw her beside the yellow Dalia flower plants while she was watering them. Rinchen kept solving the question that how to go inside. It was a timid moment for him. Suddenly, a hand landed on his shoulder. Rinchen shook abruptly and turned back discovering her uncle Skalzang Rinchen Lonpo standing there with a smile.

Skalzang quoted, “Young man, it’s quite a surprise and contented to see you here.”

Rinchen took a second to prepare himself and said “Hello, it’s been a while since I came here, just stopped nearby.”

“Yeah, I remember, you used to come here to call Brother in law on behalf of Kalon.” Uncle Skalzang responded.

“Jemadar Chhewang Rinchen, now you turned out to be a young man since I saw you.” He further added

“You know my name?” Rinchen asked with composure and a smile. “Who doesn’t? my child!”

“Entire Ladakh is proud of you.” he said.

“Thank you very much.”, Rinchen blushed.

Chuskit Dolma noticed both his uncle and Chhewang Rinchen outside the premises, she spurred a little grin on her face.

Uncle Skalzang hosted Rinchen with a warm welcome and asked his niece to bring tea for them.

Rinchen and Chuskit both had sweet innocent eye contact for a second when she served tea.

"What brought you here, Son?" He asked firmly.

Rinchen thought for a while and it took a few seconds to conclude that he had to be straight in his words. The solider in him took charge.

By lifting his courage and voice Rinchen said, "It might sound very sudden and unexpected to you."

"Don't worry, just relax and say it," uncle Skalzang assured him.

With a deep breath and with a very humble voice Rinchen said "I like your niece with all my heart and soul; I'm asking her hand for marriage." He continued,

"I seek your blessing and permission to marry her.", Rinchen cleared his honest stand.

Uncle Skalzang was silent for a couple of minutes; after a gust of breath he said,

"We will be fortunate to have you as our son-in-law."

His words might have felt like a world-win for him, but he swiftly discovered Chuskit Dolma standing nearby and hearing them. Rinchen realised her permission was more important on this occasion. He was a gentleman.

He requested Uncle Skalzang to ask her niece. Rinchen wanted to honour her choice at foremost consideration. Again, it made him anxious in waiting for her answer.

"You do know Chhewang Rinchen very well. Will you accept his proposal?", uncle asked her opinion in front of Rinchen.

She stood silent before confirming in a nervous voice, "I accept his proposal."

An 18-year-old boy who won the war for the nation in the battleground, finally earned the hands which would hold him tightly. From a little kid going inside that house as a messenger to being the son-in-law of the house was his blessing which he discovered there. He chose his paths in profession and personal life. He followed his heart and never delayed action which made him deserve the best of everything.

One of the happiest moments in his life was when uncle Skalzang readily agreed to the marriage. The news reached later to Kalon and then to Rinchen's parents. His mother was thrilled with the news and the entire family cherished this auspicious moment.

By the next year, both families chose 1st June, 1950 as the wedding day and marriage was performed with full Tibetan Buddhist custom under the blessings of Lord Buddha ordained by Lama in Gompa of Leh. Both were below twenty years and, at that time, it was normal considering the customs. Both accepted each other as husband and wife and entered the sacred bond of marriage.

In the Buddhist custom, the wife is considered solely equal to the husband and the marriage must be honoured for entire life. Both Chhewang Rinchen and Chuskit Dolma found their love in the bond without sharing words with each other. Their eyes and heart spoke for their soul during the entire wedding ceremony. The bride was brought with full celebration and cultural ceremony to Sumur in Rinchen's ancestral home. Rinchen's mother loved her daughter-in-law as her own child.

Rinchen's life entered its most beautiful bloom after he got married. Rinchen was on leave for his wedding. His senior officers also attended the wedding.

After spending one month in Sumur, Rinchen left for Leh in July. After his arrival at Leh HQ, when Rinchen was preparing for the parade on the ground for India's third Independence Day, the HQ received a letter from Delhi. After the flag hoisting event, when the troops raised their eyes towards the waving Tricolour, the national anthem filled the air with patriotism and bliss all around Leh. After the ceremony, Rinchen was summoned by his superiors.

"Jemadar Chhewang Rinchen!", Lt. Col. P.N.Kaul lauded.

"Yes, Saabji!", Rinchen stood in attention.

"We feel proud by announcing this, you will be honoured with Mahavir Chakra for your exemplary bravery and courage during the war.", Lt. Col P.N. Kaul cited.

"I'm greatly honoured, Saabji." With hefty eyes but a swift voice Rinchen responded.

It was the moment when India got its youngest Mahavir Chakra recipient. His investiture ceremony took place after two years in Srinagar in September 1952. All India Radio hailed his name all over the nation during the gallantry commendation and quoted him as "The Youngest & Bravest JCO and Saviour of Ladakh."

Rinchen's parents, his wife, siblings, and his friends attended the ceremony in Srinagar. J&K'S then PM, Sheikh Mohammed Abdullah, pinned the medal on the chest of Jemadar Chhewang Rinchen.

The child of Nubra became the protector of the nation. The journey of a small kid to becoming youngest MVC recipient Jemadar Chhewang Rinchen is not a story but an epic which should be told and read.

❑

Chapter 6

An Enigma in the Eastern Front

In 1949, momentarily remembered as the year of tectonic shift in the global order, the Indian subcontinent saw the end of first Indo-Pak War, changing the fateful geographical line completely for the entire region. The Indian Army managed to stop Pakistani forces from taking over J&K and the vast region of Ladakh was saved from barbaric invasion. While the governing body in Central Cabinet took the breath of relief in New Delhi, 2350 miles away in Tiananmen Square the Red Dragon took the first breath of rule in dominance over the mainland China.

The Chinese Communist Party announced the creation of Communist authority over the entire country, hailing the creation of People's Republic of China under the Red Flag of Communist Revolution led by Mao Zedong. The amalgamation of major provinces to create unified China factored with an adventurous motif of Communist forces with the support of farmers and labourers in the Civil War. The redness took the entire world into an unbridled storm. The year 1949 saw as the birth of an adversary that India failed to recognise in the early days.

The echoes of the newly formed China's in-game spooked the peaceful Tibet which later turned out to be a nightmare for the administration in Lhasa. Red China called for the unification of every inch of land into one state. For the dragon, they deemed to be the rightful owners even though the geographical lines were never defined as agreed cloistered boundaries with neighbouring states even well during the monarchy and democratic rule in China. All neighbour felt the early heat waves except India.

In 1954, after five years since awakening of the sinister China, finally the dreadful dragon turned its serious stare on the South, the peaks of the Himalayas over the kingdom of Tibet, in 1951. The 17-point agreement was signed by Tibetan officials and the Central Chinese Commission which established document factored right over Tibet by the Communist China; in reality, it was a fear-plugged diplomacy. The reason for the leaders of Lhasa's denial to comply on the charter road of agreement cordially was the hidden cruel motive of Red China.

The years were filled with mourning, violence sparked after the aggression of the People's Liberation Army into the province thus igniting the Tibet Uprising in 1959. The ravaging of Tibetan land during the invasion brought the Chinese wing over the vast land of Aksai Chin ranging over various important peaks including Kailash ranges and strategic passages which made China convinced that in time of despair India could meddle its way to aid Tibet. It was no less than the carrot and stick strategy which China had begun with its foreign affairs with India foresighting the possibility and edge India held, yet China didn't want to gamble during the Tibet's crushing.

In 1956, China constructed a road through Aksai Chin connecting Xinjiang and Tibet, which ran south of the Johnson Line in many places. Aksai Chin was easily accessible by the Chinese, but the access from India, which meant negotiating the Karakoram mountains was much more difficult.

"The more chaotic the condition in Tibet becomes the better; for it will help train our troops and toughen the masses. Furthermore, the chaos will provide a sufficient reason to crush the rebellion and carry out reforms in the future." The words of Mao Zedong when Tibet rebelled to stay independent and the PLA was impaled at the heart of Lhasa.

In November 1955, estranged cold breeze flowing over the mild but sharp space of Gilgit frontier at the western mountainous terrain of Ladakh. A fair heightened man sitting on the rock a few steps away from the post with tricolour waving in the serene sight. He was viewing the stupendous scenery till the horizon reaches to the peaks away at the end roof of the sky afar. Suddenly he saw a runner boy from Leh's headquarters storming towards the post. His presence seized the serenity, rushing from the rock he started moving to the post. The runner brought some essential commodities and foremost letters sent by families. The man who ran was none other than Chhewang Rinchen.

Chhewang Rinchen, ranked as Subedar part of 7 J&K Militia, was deployed in the western edge to guard the tactical position around the ridges crossing the passage inside Gilgit to oversee the enemy positions. Rinchen's famed Nubra Guards were now permanently included in the 7 J&K Militia, although the men of the unit were under the instrumental command of Rinchen himself.

A year before in 1954, the Indian Government under PM Nehru sealed a bilateral agreement with China establishing the corridor of closer relationship under the five principles of 'Panch Sheel'. It was incorporated in the Preamble of the Agreement which directed India to have hope on peace in the future between both the Asian giants which would, later, extend to the rest of the world.

Under the false intent, the Chinese Premier managed to bring Indian Officials into a convincing newfound friendship under the new slogan in the game 'Hindi Chini Bhai Bhai'. Unfortunately, the absurdity to plot a wicked plan against the Indian territory took the foothold into the Indian Government that they failed to see through the game of the Chinese. The signing of 'Panch Sheel' was only a dubious action to keep India under the fake pretext of friendship, China needed ample time to build strategic paths to allow smooth transportation of troops and weapons and set up military installations in Tibet. The endeavour of China entered Indian territory, the road project linking Sinkiang with Tibet was expanded right inside the Aksai Chin. This was the beginning of the Dragon's first stomp over the Indian territory.

Rinchen was leading his nonnos of Nubra guards as part of the 7 J&K Militia on the foot front over the Gilgit region which once saw the first war between two new rivals on the lap of the subcontinent. The runner boy distributed letters to the soldiers, Rinchen was quite eager for his letter; he left his home for the duty in early September after finishing his holiday. Rinchen got his letter, like a curious child he quickly opened and found the letter was from his beloved wife. Subedar was inaudible for a while reading the letter, suddenly his men saw their Tiger got a vibrant smile on his face. His excited nonnos asked about the beaming reason which sparked his happiness.

"I'M GONNA BE A FATHER!", Rinchen gushed his auspicious words.

In a fraction of a moment, the entire camp echoed with delighting wishes for Rinchen. Ahead of this news, Rinchen sought the wish to go home. After assessing the region and extrapolating the condition of the defences in the region, Chhewang Rinchen got the permission from his then Commanding Officer.

Chhewang Rinchen arrived in Sumur and spent a few weeks before taking his wife to Leh to her parent's home as she wished. In early January 1956, Subedar Rinchen was summoned by HQ in Leh and ordered to retake the position with his nonnos in the western sector. Rinchen bid farewell to his wife, who was under the care of her parents, and returned to the post.

Four months later in the mid of May, Subedar Rinchen was on a vigil with his nonnos. A letter came from Leh just for him, Rinchen was nervous to open it but he peeped into the paper without wasting a second, while reading the letter he felt the jolt of happiness which rolled as tears on his cheeks. The words written on paper were fervent and cathartic for him.

One of his Nonnos asked, "Brother Rinchen, what's the news. Is everything alright?"

After gathering the delight in his words, Rinchen said, "God has blessed us with a daughter."

Not every time this happened but the nest of sentinels busted in celebration in their own way, after all those men were Rinchen's family too. After completing his duty in the upcoming months, Rinchen rushed to Leh to get a glimpse of his daughter. The mother of the newborn was waiting for her child's father.

Finally, his steps were heard from the threshold, capturing his daughter's visage was one of his most fascinating moments.

Seeing the little face, Rinchen whispered to his wife "Look I think we got your little reflection here!"

She responded, "With your grace in her presence."

The first child of Chhewang Rinchen echoed her cry to her father's ear thus directing Rinchen towards his new role as a father of an infant. The child was named Phunsog Angmo. The next year, Rinchen was blessed with another sweet daughter Dechan Angmo. The father of two daughters, the Tiger of Nubra, had realised the fact that he had young cubs to raise and protect his zeal to serve as a soldier and protector soured eventually more at zenith.

In 1957, the entire paradigm of Tibetan efforts to silence the Chinese roar came to a futile transition. As the tension was soaring high in the kingdom, the Chinese Army completed their entire network of roads slashing away inside the territory of the Indian administered region of Aksai Chin. The Indian Government discovered its existence only in 1958 after Tibet's Xinhua incident which later erupted into full-scale rebellion in 1959 resulting in the Tibetan Uprising. When the Indian Government sent two patrols to ascertain whether the road cut through the Indian territory, one of the patrols was captured and released later only on the government's request.

This was the crony act by the Chinese and it showed their intent of gulping the land. But it seems that it got washed away by the sugar-coated diplomacy of China which was nothing but a wicked enchantment of illusion. In October 1959, the Chinese Army captured a small column of policemen, nine of whom were killed and ten were taken prisoner and subjected to inhuman treatment. It was then they slowly showed their claws behind their backs. As the year and the decade came to an end, the dragon managed to spread its thorns over west and south of the Aksai Chin through the network of roadways allowing passage to transport the desired number of troops and established new posts disregarding India's protests. In the noise of political slogans, the boots efforts were silenced.

Enlightened actual reality was uncovered during Premier Chou En-lai's visit to India. While the address, he coldly and sharply defended PLA's action by claiming the territory occupied by China as theirs and it was no intrusion or aggression. Indian diplomats got splashes of water on their face. India disclosed the truth, ironically which was known by every solider earlier itself that "Bhai" what India gleefully called "Chinis" were nonetheless wolves in the cloak of sheep. A new enemy flaunted its fang that day, the snake sitting on the shoulder of Himalayas hissed towards India's naive humility after coiling up the entire Aksai Chin. So far, it was the paramilitary under the Home Ministry that had the responsibility of the security of the borders in this region. Dispensing the course of the decision was already late but finally in April 1960, the responsibility of guarding the borders in Ladakh was handed over to the Indian Army and for the first time, the Indian Army set its foot into the vast high plains of Ladakh.

The summits of prominence in the Himalayas forcibly wakened from the century-old deep slumber. The ancient mountainous passages that once saw historical moments once again prepared to witness a modern time upfront conflict. It was a long frontal lane of 500 km that a vigil against Chinese intrusions into Indian territory had to be maintained if they wanted to assert dominance. The Indian Government brutally failed to understand the strategy of China about the intention of occupying territory by military adventuring. The aftermath was resulted in playing along with the Chinese the game of clash to balance the manoeuvres. The political dogma certainly had its failure to outflank the enemies. The Indian Army had to edge as far forward as possible to assert its territorial rights, with lesser ongoing support and lack of supply chain of logistics.

The doctrinal change was observed with orders emanated from the Government of India in pursuance of the new 'Forward Policy' to be implemented by the Armed Forces deployed in the desolate inhospitable heights along the extensive border. The summits ranging beyond the channelling of Indian forces' reach had a severe implication for the sudden course of establishing the post. It was only one Brigade, that too 'under armed', which had to implement insurmountable orders. It could only set up small isolated points, some of them barely consisting of 10 to 20 strong, whereas the Dragon had its numerous nests waiting for the reaction of our forces. They were expecting us since the day their premier made a skull rattling statement regarding the Aksai Chin.

The feeling of despair was already mounting over the north and it came waving over the Indian soil. In early 1959, Chhewang Rinchen was a Subedar in 7 J&K Militia Ladakhi and was deployed at Batalik in the Gurgurdo sector. The ties between

India and China dipped at low and an unexpected update reached to the ears that the Chinese had ambushed a patrolling unit in an area close to the Hot Springs in Chang Chenmo. During the active duty, Rinchen was ordered to report to the Headquarters at Leh, he was called back. He rushed walking with his nonnos and covered the distance within 4 days, which normally took 7 days, on the blizzard time with hardship; perseverance coursed through his veins.

Getting into a tough call to report in minimal time, the unit arrived with Subedar Rinchen. He stayed in Leh for two days but on the last day of his presence, he faced the stone on heel situation with the then Commanding Officer who put forth the orders for an inspection of his company on the Parade Ground. Subedar Rinchen predicted what would later happen, nevertheless he instructed his Company to stand on one side of the Zorawar Fort ground.

When the Commanding Officer initiated the inspection on the ground, he discovered that most of Rinchen's men were wearing torn shirts and trousers and about half of them were wearing 'pabu' shoes instead of ammunition boots that enraged the CO seeing the unit in disordered condition. Moreover, most of them had long, inappropriate hair. The Commanding Officer shouted in rage and ordered Rinchen for a punishment march back and told him to take the Company on a 'route march' to Pnyang Nullah and then come back doubling. Everyone noticed that Rinchen denied accepting the suddenly-concluded punishment. Indeed, Rinchen was furious too but he balanced his composure well in front of the CO.

The clash of eyes and spear stroking of argued words from both the sides led Rinchen demanding an urgent and straight talk with the Commanding Officer. The Adjutant denied him the interview and told him to fall back since the talk could be arranged only when he came back after the route march. Rinchen required an answer about the sudden punishment discharged by the CO that made him more persistent and insisted on being taken to the Commanding Officer. When the Commanding Officer agreed to interview him, he properly saluted him with his Sten gun 'slung' but expressed that he would not order his men to march. With curious-rage the Commanding Officer asked him the reason for not carrying out the orders. Rinchen gutted out his reasons and explained that numerous letters and signals had been sent for resupply of clothing and request for barbers and cobblers but HQ had shown no intention to address the demands.

After being rationally asked about a haircut of his own, Subedar explained that zero cuts of hair among the Buddhists were done only when their parents died, as per the Buddhist Culture. Being a robust willed soldier and ardent Buddhist, Rinchen kept his duty toward both the customs, he never disturbed one for another.

After listening to his reasons, the Commanding Officer, however, remained unfazed and denied cancelling his orders. After receiving resistance in the mounting moment by Rinchen, CO expressed to push off his order of preventing Rinchen's permanent commission in the military. It sounded threatening to Rinchen, as the CO was stubborn, Subedar Rinchen was also in a persistent mood, and after listening to the CO he laid aside his Sten gun and told his Commanding Officer that he would not serve anymore. Feeling the heat of the moment, Subedar Major Chhosphel tried to convince Rinchen to abide by the orders of the Commanding Officer but Rinchen was not in a state to surrender to the words. The Major feared to lose an incredible soldier over a trivial matter but after a couple of hours ultimately, it was decided that Subedar Rinchen would punish his Company in whatever way he wanted and he was asked to take the gun back. Major took breath of relief over the tall. He stood with his men at all cost. He understood the ground reality. He knew the story of every man under him. It was not just his courage which made him one of the finest soldiers in the Indian Army.

Subedar Rinchen went to the parade ground and addressed the jawans, "You will be punished as per orders. Saavdhan, follow me." As soon as they reached the cemetery approximately 300 metres away from the parade ground, he gave a long whistle and ordered his jawans to double back to the Zorawar Fort. In return, he warned his nonnos to be well-disciplined soldiers in future. Seeing Rinchen's ability to command his word, in later days the CO admired Rinchen's characteristics.

New uniforms and ammunition boots were issued by the Quarter Master in the Headquarters and they were given leave to go home before proceeding for the next mission. In the course of a glimpse, the entire scenario was grilled with indiscipline and resistance against the authority by Rinchen. But it cannot be denied that there was a lacklustre effort from the side of the staff providence too.

Resulting in the Commanding Officer's softer reaction since then, Rinchen's well-meaning intensions were understood. After a deep observation, the CO found Rinchen a man of honour for his soldiering qualities. During the departure of the CO next day for the south-east of Ladakh, the Senior Officer tweaked Rinchen in sarcasm and asked him to send a special type of stick from Dungti, when Rinchen asked 'why', he replied "to deal with people like you." Rinchen smirked in laughter and saluted him by saying, "Sir, most certainly."

Rinchen put everyone in comfort by again pointing to the normalising of the matter. Subsequently, Subedar Chhewang's Company was ordered to move to Dungti and Chushul in the southern sector within 24 hours to establish posts at Dungti, Demchok, Kuyul, and Chushul. After covering a long distance of 201 km, his Company, with a big load on a backpack basis, he and his men reached Dungti in 13 days of a long and harsh journey.

After reaching the point, out of nowhere the soldier had to create the perimeter out of scratch in sub-zero degree temperature. It was no easy job to bring essentials back up after 13 days of footwork and set up the post in a place that was never a site. Finally, the unit required to prepare bunkers, at least three for each platoon, for which they had to get Ballis (Bamboos), corrugated iron sheets, doors, and windows. To ease them, the Indian Air Force came to the rescue. All the essentials were airdropped and construction took two to three months to complete. Entire survival was dependent upon a single source of essential during the patrolling days. Thereafter, they had to depend upon airdropped rations and supply of arms and armaments. Entire airdropping of resources was held on fixed days, at scheduled times, the Platoons were focused on the sky for helicopters bringing the required commodities and particularly letters from home. This was the only way of hope to live and carry duty in abundance. In addition, all the months they never skipped their patrol routines to keep vigil and monitor the potential moment of Chinese, plus to observe the possibility of encroachment upon Indian soil and establishment of their routed posts.

Upon these terrains devilish blizzard made each night a frozen hell for Chhewang Rinchen and his men. It seriously took these brave souls to be warm in this ruthless environment with only little material elements and sheer infinite will, Rinchen spent around 8 months in the area from October 1959 to June 1960, being the active eyes at forwarding helm for the Indian Forces.

After the horrific choking of Lhasa by the PLA at the yearend in 1959, later in 1960, ultimately intelligence flinched about Chinese penetration in the northern sector. It was nonetheless a wolf stepping in the blizzard. Rinchen's presence in the Nubra Sector became more important as only the child of the mountain would be able to navigate into the laps of the icy dimensions. In June 1960, Subedar Rinchen was transferred from 7 J&K Militia Ladakhi to 14 J&K Militia Ladakhi, the newly raised battalion. After taking charge of a new company in Spituk Dak Bungalow in Leh, he was ordered to move with a Company to the Nubra

Sector Deskit to relieve Major Chand Singh who, till then, was the Sector Commander in Shyok Wing. After transferring to the sector, he felt the levitation of his orders as it was his first command for a Company in the role of a Commissioned Officer (as a Second Lieutenant). The post was surely energised to carry out tactical reconnaissance which was his first task after reaching there.

The Indian Army needed a landing strip to expand its availability of the forces in the northwest since Ladakh was an unfamiliar land to them. This was the first mission Rinchen became associated with. The task during his stay in the sector was to oversee the construction of an airfield at Thoise. This was the first airstrip to be built in the northwest region of Ladakh and the second in Ladakh. The first had been built at Leh in 1948. The actionable moment was unreal to witness; the local Nubra people carried the load of work to build the airstrip at Thoise with their free services. Capt. Bajwa of the Engineers was detailed to supervise the construction work, while Mr. K.D. Menon who was the Assistant Commissioner Deskit gave all possible assistance, particularly in the supply of wheat yeast for making chhang (local beer) which was distributed free of cost to all those volunteers who were fond of it. Chhang was an essential commodity and above-board demand since the habitat of outskirts of Ladakh was unfavourable due to extreme cold. Chhang helped to preserve the heat of the body. The non-Buddhists of Baigdangdo were served local tea, 'gurgur butter tea', for which a few mounds of wheat were allotted for the purchase of tea and butter. The people of Nubra took the entire construction on their shoulders in the bidding of Rinchen. The entire construction was done on war-footing and the volunteers worked even during the night with the help of petromax light which was the only easygoing source of light during the yesteryears.

After 3 months of sheer head to heel space work-shift, by September 1960, the airfield, which was at a height of 3,500 metres, was ready. The landing of transport aircraft was eligible to land on 26th September; IAF landed the first Dakota turboprop tactical airlifted on the airfield piloted by Sqn. Ldr. C.K-S. Raje (later Retd as Air Marshal). He was accompanied by Air Vice Marshal Pinto. In the beginning of 1961, 14 J&K Militia (Ladakhi) were moved to the north and its Headquarters were not established at Partapur. It was feared that the Chinese who had already penetrated along the Chip Chap River might occupy Daulat Beg Oldi before the Indians would reach. Daulat Beg Oldi was the transitional outpost for India; it was a despicable lantern in a sense for security forces. The region was named Daulat Beg Oldi after the name of a Yarkandi merchant, Daulat Beg, who was caught in a blizzard and died there. The place was situated 16 km to the south of the Karakoram Pass, Daulat Beg Oldi rested in the deep snow-capped wilds of the Depsang plains, at an altitude of 5,000 metres.

From Leh, the region measured at 120 km on the silk trade route between Leh and Yarkand. There were two routes from Leh to Daulat Beg Oldi: one which would go via river Shyok, the winter route and the other which would go across Saser La, the summer route. Both converged at the Murgo point ahead. The entire area between Murgo, which was known as 'Gateway to Hell', and Daulat Beg Oldi was famed for ruthless weather and snowstorm. Beyond this region, the Indian policymakers didn't have much clue to outline the surrounding, losing Daulat Beg Oldi would mean losing the gates of Northeast Ladakh.

Indian Army Mountain Corps started their respective dreadnought skill honing in the high summits. No wonder Indian forces later became the crown of mountain warfare in the world, by 1961 young Lieutenant Chhewang Rinchen came under the fortunate wings of a prominent expert in mountain warfare, Major S.S. Randhawa (later Lt. Col). The struggle of the mountain was no child's play and Major Randhawa was skilled in the toughest mountain warfare and had treasure of knowledge regarding combating missions in the harsh and hellish regions. Even though he was not a blooming flower of Ladakh but he had well pollinated his expertise within his history of memorable years of the first Indo-Pak confrontation of 1947-48 when he was a Staff Officer to Colonel H.S. Parab. The unspeakable wartime transcended his love for the mountain over the zeal of affection. There he cultivated an obsession for the icy winds, snow blizzards and snow-capped peaks of Ladakh. In his second tenure as a Major (second-in-command) in 14 J&K Militia, he had been the first Indian Army Officer to make surveillance up to the Karakoram Pass as early as 1960. When the Indian Army adopted the forward Policy in the region, he did a spearhead of intelligence gathering for the forces with his mates.

Rinchen remembered his words for Randhawa in his deep memories that he owed a lot to well-directed instructions given by him. He was followed strictly while going out on reconnaissance missions on the uncharted wilderness of the Depsang Plains and desolate heights beyond; Rinchen evolved under his words and teachings. In August 1961, in pursuance of the Forward Policy, Lt. Rinchen received the first order to carry reconnaissance in the area at extreme north and establish a post at Daulat Beg Oldi, within a stone throw from the Karakoram. The critical time exploded to endure since everyone had a hunch about Chinese inclusion in deep Aksai Chin and they didn't want to let the Daulat Beg Oldi sliding in the hands of Chinese who had gone berserk to undertake the Indian territory in name of their expansion motives. Retracing the ancient path, the old Central Asian Silk Trade Route, Rinchen, along with one NCO, one signalman, two jawans and one cook proceeded towards Daulat Beg Oldi (DBO) on a foot-walk manpack basis. Nearly six ponies were used on simpler terms for carrying ration, ammunition, and bedding. The team had a wireless set which was the only means at their disposal to keep in contact with the rest of the world. The movement had no less risk than a pack of snow leopards moving in blizzards.

This was a time of impending and brutal winter. The season had arrived; march was extremely difficult with horrendous chilly days and nights. When the team reached Saser La, Tutialak, they took a while to rest in the tiny base, warmed up themselves, and briefed the orders to the base officer. The team spent two days before crossing the Saser La. To ensure rerouting towards the destination, Rinchen, along with L/Nk Panchok Stobdan and one Sepoy climbed a summit close by, reaching the height of 6,000 metres, without any equipment and oxygen cylinders.

It was no amusing activity for children of Ladakh, every person born in the lap of Himalayas knew how to climb the prominence of mountains. The saying was not written without authentication that who should teach the fish how to swim. They reached the peak by noon and planted a Buddhist flag, "Tarchok' with the prayer 'Om mane padme hum' meaning, 'Praise to the Jewel in the Lotus' written on it, Rinchen remembered the sacred chant that when he was in his childhood, he used to hear the words in every festival echoing from adjacent Gompa. After spending a few minutes at the top, the small party returned to the base. The next morning, the whole party started climbing Saser La. After crossing Saser La, they proceeded towards Daulat Beg Oldi. At the time DBO was the deadly, souring, and highly treacherous region; many men in past had lost the path. There was a reason, beyond in the clutches of blizzards, they encountered skeletons of human beings and animals lying scattered all along the track till the line of sight.

After reaching the point, in September 3, 1961, Chhewang Rinchen stepped ahead with a patrol party, around the shores of the 'Chip Chap' river. He felt a hunch of a human preemie in the region by observing the area and they were not much old like on the second day, he noted the hoof marks of camels and horses and, a little further, tyre marks of a three-tonne vehicle. It clearly indicated the possible presence of the Chinese in the region and he concluded on the case that if tyre marks were there then the Chinese could have constructed roads deep within Indian territory and they were planning to grab Indian administered vicinity into their grip.

Wasting no time, along with three jawans, Rinchen moved ahead to locate the Chinese post, leaving his ponies and administrative tail behind on the very first day of arrival. The team had to pass through difficult terrain, this was something of a testing situation as Rinchen and the team had to crawl umpteen kilometres. in snow to reach close to the Chinese water point. Beyond the point, he climbed a small plateau to have a better glance of the enemy with his binoculars.

Reaching the vantage point of monitoring, Rinchen immediately observed less than 500 metres away from own position; the Chinese had established their regional headquarters in a double-storied fort, having two doors and many loopholes. It was a swift clarity about the battalion sized force that was present there with supply routes established for the fulfilment of needful resources.

About 300 Chinese were in the rush of making bricks and loading and unloading materials from trucks. Rinchen realised the necessity to carry the message to the HQ.

The message was immediately passed on to the Sector Headquarters, through which the message was communicated to the higher authority; the line of communication continued till it reached the Army Headquarters in New Delhi. The scenario was literally unexpected. Nobody believed that the Chinese could have penetrated deeply into that area and fortified the region as their own sovereignty. The encroaching-development of enemies proliferated twofold a year back when India had sheltered the Dalai Lama which provoked the anger of Communist China.

The presence of the fort was later verified by two Canberra fighter planes tasked for airborne reconnaissance, who took photographs of the position. Finally, the inference justified the context of the true intentions of the Chinese.

It became compulsory for the Indian Army to establish a post in the region of Despang plains. Without any delay, Rinchen and his party reached Daulat Beg Oldi and met 2nd Lt. Rathore who was informed of the establishment of a Chinese post nearby and was warned to be alert. To carry out extensive patrolling. Rinchen was ordered to stay at Daulat Beg Oldi as 2nd Lt. Rathore was about to go on leave. 2nd Lt. Rathore thus was waiting to be relieved from his post and Rinchen remained there. In October, another platoon commanded by 2nd Lt. Abdul Rahim arrived to relieve the platoon commanded by 2nd Lt. Rathore. Rathore was sent back on the backload ponies to the Headquarters at Partapur. After observing the region for one month, in December 1961, Rinchen was relieved of his duties at DBO and was flown in a helicopter to Partapur for another assignment waiting for him. Rinchen's quick assessment of the region gave the HQ a pure picture of the Chinese incursion. Rinchen took the harsh walk and completed his duty; amid he was blessed with the third daughter a month ago on 30th November 1961. Chuskit Dolma was a woman of strength when Rinchen had been in the line of duty; she carried the heaviness of his boots on her shoulders. She knew the truth that the nation needed him more than she would do. She overcame the absence of Rinchen during all three children's birth. Though Rinchen was far, his heart beat had been around the family always. The tigress had honoured the Tiger's pride for carrying his responsibility and when he arrived later, they both named their daughter Tundup Dolma following the Buddhist custom in the gompa. All three kids were named through complete custom under the blessings of Lama.

After reaching Partapur in early 1962, Rinchen was included in one of the most important and longest reconnaissance missions, his company formed consisting of Major Randhawa, Lieutenant Rinchen, along with an engineer, Captain D.S.R. Sahni (later retired as Lt.Gen.) and 15 other ranks, 17 porters and employing 40 ponies/yaks. In March, the company left Partapur and headed along the Shyok River to reach Sultan Chhushku after 15 days of a long walk. From there they followed the course of an uncharted river to enter the Sumdo Valley. No words to describe the difficulty of the path, at some extent they had to cut through the rocky area. On the way, they discovered two passes which they named 'Rinchen La' and 'Sahni La' to identify the route passage through them. A spring discovered by Subedar Bodhraj was named after him as 'Bodh Chumik'. On reaching Sumdo after a march taking another 15 days, they established a post opposite to one that was set up by the Chinese in the Aksai Chin area. This post was systematised at a height of around 4,998 metres and it was named as Jiwan Post.

As the journey from Sultan Chhushku to Sumdo was on a great height, it was open to strong gales and snow blizzards. Rinchen's company led by Major Randhawa faced a great course of peril; especially the absence of supplies was forthcoming through airdropping. Because the death of 70 per cent of the pack animals due to hypothermia caused by extreme coldness and inhospitable weather. Thus, no replacement was available for carrying the resources, the system of supplying logistic turned out one of the factors of failures in the battle of terminating Chinese on the bay. This was the condition in almost every latent edge border of Aksai Chin.

It was noted that the company cannot use the assessed old route hence they needed a short and unmapped route to DBO; hence Major Randhawa was tasked and detailed Rinchen during surveillance to find out the shortest route between Sumdo and DBO. Rinchen got split from the company and Randhawa called for rendezvous on DBO.

Rinchen agreed and proceeded on the mission along with a coolie named Nurbu of Khalsar when the dusk touched the land on a manpack basis. It was no easy venture to go on an uncharted and unmapped course to trace the new foot line for a shortcut, after walking throughout the day and most of the night; they reached a steep mountain at a height of 6,400 metres which were all covered with deep snow. Rinchen and his mate had to spend a night there as they could not navigate the proper direction to DBO during the day. For dinner, they only had the sattu with cold water which Nurroo got after breaking the ice. Soldiers living in the terrains survived in such unfathomable conditions only with their will to be alive to fight for the nation. They knew any death in between would go in vain. When Rinchen had opened his eyes to see the sky, he discovered that they were sleeping close to a Chinese post. The post was named 'Kidney Post' due to the area's elegance to be a junction of both sides of the Indian marked post. After noticing the Chinese, Rinchen changed his direction to reach another Indian post at Jagmag. The next day, they left Jagmag to reach DBO. The distance between Sumdo and DBO was 48 km and they took 2 days to cover it. After about a week, Randhawa also reached DBO through a longer route and was impressed by Rinchen's presence of mind and the ability to navigate in such conditions like a snow leopard knows the snowpath. The child of the serene mountains was also the reckoning of the dreadful blizzards and he kept reminding everyone why his abilities in such impossible conditions were never doubted and WOULD NEVER BE DOUBTED.

❑

Chapter 7

A Regret in his Heart

The strain of scenarios was mounting in the head of higher authorities, China was not ceasing the march to establish their grip on Indian soil. Crossing every day without China's influence became a feat. In the middle of 1962, the Chinese had created several posts in the Indian territory that turned to be an implied act of mocking by Communist. They sugar-coated us with betrayal. Rinchen's task turned more and more obligatory. He began to rush from place to place to find out where the Chinese had infiltrated and occupied Indian territory. Later he accomplished the task of establishing an Indian check-post opposite to the post that was set up in the Indian territory, of the Chinese. Rinchen was a soldier who acted as a multi-spectrum adaptive person of the region. His skills of one time observing and reporting the accurate picture of the scenario helped the higher officials to draw out the necessary outcomes of it.

In a span of two months, Rinchen and his reconnaissance unit reported the twofold increase of Chinese posts from April 1961 to June 1962, the number of posts increased from 13 to 65 despite of deprived 'defence potentials'. At best, they could be called 'Flag Posts', yet the posts were not to be underestimated as they served as a point of triangulation for PLA Western

Command to navigate the entire territory of Aksai Chin freely. Even though the region was rightfully India's, according to Johnson Line, China was the one who had occupied it with a network of the military establishment right under our nose. On our side, the maximum number of jawans were 125 at Daulat Beg Oldi which was not even proper battalion sized, while the minimum number of posts was five in Parmodak. Rinchen's Company Headquarters with a section of 3" mortar was moved to Chandni Post with the potential of fire exchange. Rinchen knew very well that after the area exploitation, Chinese troops would massacre aggressively.

In that northern region since the atmosphere prevented soldiers from moving for a logistic rerun, it was essential to overcome the difficulty of transportation by constructing an airfield through volunteer labour of jawans. Squadron Leader Raje landed the first aircraft, a Packet, on July 23, 1962, on the airstrip. Randhawa was puzzled about the signalling of his landing, the marking of the airfield had to be done but with what provision elevated a question in Randhawa's mind. But soon, he witnessed Rinchen was marking the airstrip with a massive number of Jerry cans and skeletons of human beings and animals which lay scattered in the region as a reminiscence of the tragedies that had taken place decades back.

For nearly half the year, Lt. Rinchen remained in constant movement of carrying out reconnaissance. Moreover, playing the role of HUMINT with an addition of establishing posts at preeminent heights. After July 1962, his role became more prominent and he got engaged in combative encounters, although it was for a minimal scale. Rinchen was the one who constantly approached the perimeters of Chinese bases and he moved from one post to another. His nerves got the strength of iron that nothing could shake him. It was him who made entire authority aware about Chinese movement in Aksai Chin with his recce ops.

On one occasion, which turned to be the first close encounter between forces during the first week of July 1962, Rinchen was leading a patrol unit and later reached at Bona Post. Unexpectedly, through wireless a message was received from Bhujang Post signalling that the Chinese had ambushed the Indian unit headed by Jemadar Tara Singh at that post. The numbers of Chinese were huge enough to force Tara Singh's unit to retreat. They were able to escape but at the cost of a few ponies loaded with signal equipment and other stores. The Indian side was already not enough armed and underpowered with a little resource. Rinchen realised the state of emergency and turned to Bhujang Post with a fighting patrol; he proceeded to Bhujang.

On the way, he found Chinese troops hiding in a Nullah to distort the Indian communication with Bhujang, thus planning to capture the post. Rinchen sought an idea and led his men to divert in a different direction with the intention of attaining an elevated position on higher ground. But the Chinese caught them and opened automatic fire on Rinchen's men. At the right moment, Rinchen took a safe distance for defence and loaded outrage of fire with his party. In the meantime, some reinforcements arrived from Bona Post to the rescue of Rinchen and covered them to force the Chinese side to run away. In the encounter, the Chinese suffered heavy losses and withdrew carrying their dead men along with equipment and logistics including some jeeps, which were also airdropped, were lost in action. They lost most of their strappings which gave them the appearance of mess-tins rather than jeeps that to be named as mess-tin jeeps, this resulted in a successful resistance from the Ladakh frontier that day and it was repeated faithfully by 14 J&K Militia Ladakhi.

It was not the culmination; the Dragon surely retreated but places like Razeng La were silently waiting for unexpected doom in a few months. On 21st July, a distress message came from Chandni Post that a patrol led by Subedar Sonam Stobdan had been attacked by the Chinese troops. It turned into blazing gunfire from both the sides and it had been in progress. Rinchen was ordered to head to Chandni Post to provide reinforcement to Sonam's party. Getting into a mess-tin jeep with six ORs and one LMG mounted in the centre, Rinchen without wasting a fraction of second stormed towards Chandni Post but got a halt just to observe before marching into the middle of fire. Through binoculars from a distance, he could observe three camels with loads and a few Chinese entering Indian territory. Rinchen raced the jeep with the object of capturing them but soon he noticed the difference in the scene. On reaching the spot, he found the camels standing on the road loaded with signal and wireless equipment.

Rinchen got the hunch through his keen power of observation and concluded that a portion of the Chinese soldiers were camouflaged behind some low bushes, aiming their automatic rifles at his party in a short-range around 20 yards. Rinchen took no chance to distract them; he just called out "hullo" multiple times and waved his hand. After distracting them Rinchen raced like a lightning bolt to Chandni Post. During the blazing run, he faced firing from the Chinese who were lying positioned behind the bushes as well as from the hills on the right. With extreme difficulty, he succeeded in extracting himself from the ambush attack and the credits went to the mess-tin jeep that successfully crossed the place.

In the gateway frontier over Chandni Post which was commanded by Subedar Rigzin Phunchok, PLA troops managed to occupy an adjacent hill in the shadow of silence in the Indian territory. Enemies were surrounding the region that closed the escape window for our troops present there. The party led by Sonam Stobdan was still fighting with the Chinese. No less than 60 to 70 Chinese had surrounded the Subedar and his patrol. Rinchen reached the location and brought his jeep to the close. As soon as he had the Chinese within his LMG firing range, Rinchen discharged his entire firepower on the Chinese, killing a few. In return, Rinchen and his unit faced firing from the hills till they were just dropped into the darkness. In midst of the firing, Rinchen needed a passage to go helping his mates, Rinchen finally found a Nullah gap, through which he stormed to help Subedar Sonam Stobdan and his men, after tedious effort and resisting enemy firing, he rescued them to safety. In the clash, Naik Tirath Singh was hit by the Chinese and broke his arms.

His unit carried him safely out of the firing range.

After rescuing Sonam and his men, he noticed something weird. To assess the scenario, he stepped differently from the unit and perceived that the Chinese were in pursuit of occupying a point 5,988 metres overlooking the DBO airfield. The point would have given the Chinese great leverage to monitor Indian movement, Rinchen rushed to counterbalance them and decided to establish a post higher than that point. From the top, he could see the Chinese moving, thus enabling the upper hand over the enemy. Soon after realising that the Indians had established a post on higher ground than them, the Chinese had no option but to retreat. Temporarily but the Chinese movement was halted. After ensuring the defences and predicting the PLA's resort of action in the upcoming months, Rinchen took a breath freely. During the skirmishes, Rinchen received a letter from Leh that her wife was ill, after serving longer than usual in the year 1962, in September he proceeded on leave from DBO as HQ granted his request. Rinchen was on and off from Leh and he barely met his wife and kids. But this time, he spent three weeks with his wife and kids. Soon after Chuskit Dolma's health improved Lt.Chhewang Rinchen was called back.

Three weeks leave went in a flash, he had returned and headed to the southeast region of Ladakh after receiving further orders. He rushed to where posts had been established earlier Kuyul, Demchok and other places. Rinchen was attached to 7 J&K Militia Ladakhi as a Subedar from October 1959 to June 1960. Rinchen served with the battalion since his first day of service during the 1948 Indo-Pak War.

Rinchen noticed the situation which had just gotten worse. To get the ground situation understood, Rinchen first went to Kuyul and Demchok to meet the officers and men of his old battalion, 7 J&K Militia. It was at Kuyul, the Battalion Headquarters of 7 J&K Militia where Rinchen was enlightened with the entire picture, on October 21, 1962, that the Chinese had brutally attacked and overrun the DBO Post. Indian side took the heavy losses but HQ didn't know the entire on-ground situation. It was dark for them especially the exact casualties and number of missing soldiers. The Commanding Officer of 7 J&K Militia also informed him that there was an order for Rinchen from the Corps Commander asking him to report immediately. Rinchen's services were needed most desperately this time. His sense of observation and judgement were required. Rinchen felt the heat of the scenario and he took the understanding that the flames would be fanned to engulf the entire Aksai Chin.

Before departing to meet the Corps Commander, he thought it was best to talk with his old friends in 7 J&K Militia, at least over the telephone. Subedar Ishe Tundup was the Post Commander at Changla.

Rinchen first took a breath and said, "It's been ages brother."

"Brother Rinchen?" Ishe asked.

"Yes, It's me."

"Brother, how's the situation at the post?" He further asked.

"Honestly? Not better, the Chinese are just raiding like hell got lose.", Ishe hushed.

"You'll be fine right?", Rinchen has shown concern.

"I can't promise that Brother, but I promise, me and my platoon are prepared to put up a tough fight even against a battalion of the Chinese.", Ishe sparked his words.

Rinchen froze for a while and replied "Just be sure to be safe and Yes! I believe you."

"Learned from the best, brother!" Ishe spoke.

"Each one of you is the best reason why our homeland is safe." Rinchen replied with pride.

"I'll assure you, I will never retreat", "Will fight till the last man and the last round.", Ishe whispered his final word before ending the call.

Rinchen was silent; it took time to digest the words even after the conversation. The words stamped in his deep memories and still they reek with deep emotion and anguish as his dear friend honoured his words and fought till the last round. As this news later reached Rinchen, his soul called for raiding all the Chinese posts on Indian soil.

Rinchen was redirected to Chushul. One morning of October 1962, Rinchen reached Chushul airfield where he met Lt. Col. Hari Chand of 2/8 GR whom he had met in the Nubra Valley fifteen years back during the Indo-Pak confrontation, 1947-48. Old memories of the Nubra Valley campaign were once more fresh and vivid. They talked about past including the raid over Gilgit post like bada khana. During the nostalgic conversation Rinchen came to know that heavy fighting was in motion in Srijap and Yulla Sectors and they are on the brink of falling into enemies' hands.

Lt. Gen Bikram Singh asked Rinchen to come with him to Srinagar HQ to brief on the DBO. Before Rinchen could take off with his superior, news arrived on the wireless that the DBO Post had been declared 'Red', to say in a civil way, the post is in grip of the enemy now. The Corps Commander revised his orders and directed him to accompany him to Leh on 23rd October.

Before proceeding to Leh, Rinchen went to the residence of His Holiness Lama Kushuk Bakula, he was, then, the Minister of Ladakh Affairs in the J&K Government but he had left already for Leh. Wondering how to approach his locals like in the 1948 war, Rinchen got a tip that Rigzin Namgial and his party were staying at a hotel. Rinchen rushed to the hotel, he found that senior leaders were having a discussion with the local businessmen, Government servants and students to draw the possible defensive plan of action for Ladakh. Rinchen's arrival astonished everyone that his appearance showed that he had not been killed in action at Chandni Post. It was believed that the entire company along with him had been wiped off by the Chinese. After a few minutes, the entire hall galvanised with Rinchen's name hailing. Seeing Rinchen and embracing him by turns were cherished. Also, the raising slogan, 'Rinchen Zindabad' perplexed as well as amazed Rinchen who had no idea of what was happening. Once the josh settled down, he made everyone comfortable and suggested forming committees of the Ladakhis to cooperate with the Army and do all necessary for intensifying war efforts to fight the Chinese's aggression and protect the Ladakh at all force and will.

On the morning of 23rd October, during a high official conference, the Corps Commander gave details of the military situation in the presence of Brigadier T.N. Raina and His Holiness Kushuk Bakula of Ladakh and called for humble and determined support by the civilian population for the defence of the country. His Holiness Bakula assured the Commander on behalf of Ladakh that the full support of the people belongs to the Army.

During the detailed conference, Rinchen sparked with an idea. It was just like earlier times when he had raised Nubra Guards. He offered his services to raise and train a battalion of Karakoram Guards to support the Army to tackle the Chinese aggression. The Corps Commander impressed and accepted the proposal with an immediate notice; further, they agreed to supply arms by air transportation for the Karakoram Guards in the Nubra Valley. The Brigade Commander gave a helicopter to Rinchen for his early arrival to the place and His Holiness Kushuk Bakula also accompanied him to visit the Nubra Valley for war efforts. While flying towards the location, Rinchen asked the pilot of the helicopter make a halt at Sumur where from Rinchen's father, Kunzang Dorje who was the President of the Nubra Valley unit of the National Congress also joined them to help in raising the Karakoram Guards. He didn't stop in Sumur for personal work but for his duty which was admired by many silently.

Rinchen's father was an influencer and he had his son's back while raising Nubra Guards, From Sumur they flew to Deskit and raised an initial force of a thousand who were coaxed and motivated by Rinchen and His Holiness Bakula. Rinchen sparked and ignited the rows of desire in young people to fight for the land. Rinchen had the superior skill of convincing people with honour and determination. His ability to command a novice group and transform them into a fighting force was timely tested which had been witnessed in the past.

The training of the force would be commenced after the arrival of promised arms and ammunition. To transport them, 300 porters and 300 ponies were also brought into motion. Many helping hands came to assist Rinchen's effort. To emphasis, the appreciable help was given by the Assistant Commissioner of the Nubra Valley. When a large proportion of young blood joined the Karakoram Guards, the wise old men and women who were unable to serve in combat offered to supply rations for the newly raised force. In the period of rumble, to save the homeland every breath of Nubra and Ladakh used to flame the young soldiers into the forge of Army. Thus, proved the utmost loyalty and uncalled patriotism from the humble people of Ladakh. Chhewang Rinchen was the beacon of the willpower of people who became a pioneer to carry the safety of the land on his shoulders without frowning about the resources. The sane deed of people showed the world, what Indians were capable of. After independence, India was in the phrase of standing in its own leg, but the efforts of people escalated the stamina to run even before walking. This was written in the history of India to show all of us that India is our motherland; never expect anyone to protect it; volunteer when time calls.

After the initial month of training and before the force could receive arms and ammunition to make it an effective fighting scout to aid Armed forces, Rinchen was ordered to proceed towards the DBO post along the Shyok river with the remnants of 14 J&K Militia to stop the advances of the Chinese. Because the main force with the Commanding Officer and the Second-in-Command were reported missing after the fall of the DBO post, Rinchen didn't wish to leave but seeing an honest effort from everyone to raise the guard, he convinced himself to march.

It was again a foot walk, long march along with his Company. Rinchen left the Sector Headquarters, on October 24, 1962, to reach the Shyok village in October 27. Extreme and exhausting long march covering 130 km which included the crossing, of Tangyar La Peak passage didn't break him and his men. At Shyok, a message arrived from the Brigade Commander to put up a defence position at Chong Jangal, since the DBO was over raided by the enemy, brains in the Army had to fear that Shyok could be overrun in no time. The Army bolstered its assets to build defences around the village boundaries.

During defensive drawing in HQ by Commanders that evening, a piece of news arrived from Sultan Chhushku that the Commanding Officer and the Second-in-Command with a few jawans of 14 Ladakhi Scouts, who were missing for some time, had reached at Sultan Chhushku. About 30 per cent of the troops had been killed or were missing. Rinchen took the charge at Chandni Post, even with his company at Chandni Post and certain other posts had been overrun by overwhelming force from PLA troops. All the wounded and frostbite cases had been evacuated to Leh by helicopter. The treacherous atmosphere and incalculable events of harsh terrain made it impossible for the Indian side to match the defences against the Chinese who had been preparing for this day way before 1956.

Rinchen went to the post in a strong sense of spirit to carry offensive operations against the Chinese. He had the quest to forward with any greater or simpler opportunity when he could get a nodding to attack Chinese posts along with his Commandos on an out operation to throw out Chinese from the land and reclaim Aksai Chin. A month passed by and Rinchen just kept having a vigil of hawk-eye on the region for a sudden change in status quo at the horizon in front of DBO. However, the Indian Army superiors were busy with the Chushul front and focused on other frontiers which were thought to fall under the offensive of PLA and exactly where our side subsequently faced a debacle of an oddity. In military terms, the offensive window was missed and Chhewang Rinchen's dreams remained unfulfilled. This was one of the situations which went on to remain as a regret not to opt for a charter of offensive attack. Rinchen disliked living under the thumb of defensive strategy when the enemy himself was ready in the front gear to attack every time.

In the entire conflict narration on the ground, neither the Indian Government nor perhaps the Indian Army had foresighted that the PLA would ever choose to raid us with a prepared and brutal wave attack. When the attack came to the door front, the Indian Army was neither prepared nor completely understood the entire picture of China's intention. The attack was a spade of sudden action that certain Indian forward posts spotted white painted Chinese jeeps but failed to comprehend the latter's sinister plan. From Indian leaders to the foreign policymakers, everyone received the thorns of war inside the fake flowers of friendship which the Chinese Premier gifted us. Due to those thorns, India lost a massive chunk of strategic land while the soldier bleeding from the cut by a friend who turned as enemy which we were unaware of; The Burmese leader did warn the

Indian Government many years back but the warning was taken as a pinch of salt by our leaders.

On scale and level of offensive operations, People's Liberation Army battalions raided in the night of 19/20 October 1962, in the Permodak Post at a height of 5,485 metres and

Bishan Post at a height of 5,650 metres were overrun by about 2200 hours. To add in the list, on the same day, Chandni Post was overrun. One by one the jawans fell and Chandni Post was turned into dust. Rinchen came after a week to the post while Naib Subedar Rigzin Phunchok succeeded in retreating to Sultan Chhushku with his surviving men. Soon after, October 20, the Daulat Beg Oldi post was surrounded by Chinese troops from all sides but the post was never surrendered and the Indian Army managed to reclaim it back.

The venture of Chinese troops continued for two days, 26–27 October and when they captured Demchok, Jara La, and Chang La in south-east Ladakh. For a month, they remained silent, ground troops knew that it was silence before the storm but government leaders still wanted to believe that these were mere skirmishes carried in misadventures by Chinese troops and it was not a fullscale declared war on the sovereign nation of India. A month later China cleared the doubt from the brains of Indian leadership. The shocking attack, as we could call, it stormed us from 18–20 November the Chinese captured Rezang La, Gurung Hill, and Mugger Hill in the Chushul sector.

After raiding and killing Indian soldiers, who were unprepared for the wave due to lack of network intelligence for knowing the enemy's intention and failure to identify the wicked image of China through the foreign affairs, in November, the ruthless attack went into dark silence again. On 22nd November, the Chinese announced a unilateral ceasefire with declaring the entire Aksai Chin as their rightful sovereignty, thus successfully cutting India's large region without a flinch. The game played on the table became the reason for the death of men in uniform and for abandoning a piece of pride along with Aksai Chin.

The entire nation took a long time to recover from the betrayal and the Indian Armed Forces earned a chunk of wisdom from the wound, adding China to the list of permanent rivals. More than countable in fingers, jawans were honoured with awards on the Republic Day, January 26 in 1963. Rinchen was awarded the Sena Medal. Quite a few were posthumous awards including Rinchen's dear friend JCO Ishe Tundup who was awarded Mahavir Chakra posthumously. With deep pain in his heart, Rinchen swallowed his happiness seeing his friend receiving the honour for sacrificing his life for the nation.

The course of gutful action and head over heel operation which Rinchen did marvellously with his nonnos in 1948 war was sorely missed in the conflict against a new enemy. Rinchen knew what it took to be a solider as he learned his lessons early.

Rinchen continued his duty of reconnaissance to keep vigil over Chinese activity to be at 'edge as far forward to the Chinese post as possible'. The task involved great peril and a dangerous course of action, it was no less than throwing ourselves into the pit of death and was certainly not enough inevitable for the thrill it offered to the adventurous spirited Rinchen. His service had critical and crucial importance during the span of Sino-Indo War in 1962. Seeing unfathomable survival skills and war-fighting ability in the harsh terrains of the Himalayas equipped his mind and soul.

The Indian Army decided to raise a new unit devoted to the vast region of Ladakh. Rinchen's eye-catching service record and his nonnos and other Ladakhis' enthusiastic warfare ability gave many Commanders the impression to bring these fine warriors into the Indian Army. In 1963, Indian Army took 7 Jammu Kashmir Militia and 14th Militia with adjacent Nubra Guards warriors to form Ladakh Scouts, thus the famed Snow Leopards were born at that day.

Rinchen's qualities of an acute soldier and resilience assaulted the attention of Colonel (Later Brigadier) T.B. Kapur, who was the Sector Commander of Partapur from 1965 to mid-67. Col. Kapur trained and taught many of his subordinates but out of all Col. Kapur singled out Rinchen by the name to be called from his post and used his assistance to carry out special reconnaissance tasks beyond the enemy lines especially near to the skin as close to the enemy positions at insurmountable heights in the crucial years of 1965 where the enemy in the Western frontier were preparing for something large against India.

❑

Shri Kunzang Dorje & Smt. Jamyang Dolma the parents of Colonel Chhewang Rinchen

Shri Stanzin
Colonel Rinchen's childhood teacher

Shri Stanzin Tsering, The Headman of the Teggar Village

Shri Sonam Narboo, The man who constructed Leh Airfield in 1948

The first Dakota aircraft of Indian Air Force that landed on Leh Airfield in 1948. The people of Leh came to see the Plane with grass thinking it was a giant creature

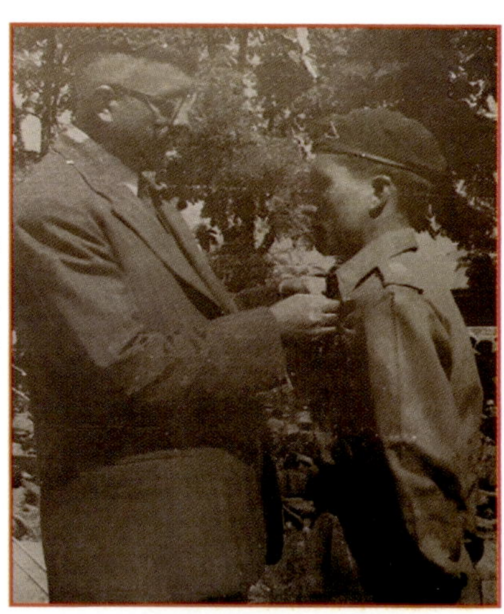

Shri Sheikh Abdullah, the then Chief Minister of Jammu & Kashmir, pinning the Mahavir Chakra on the chest of Jemadar Chhewang Rinchen

Newly married Jemadar Chhewang Rinchen & Smt. Chuskit Dolma

Father of Colonel Chhewang Rinchen, Shri Kunzang Dorje with Colonel S.S. Randhawa

Havildar Tashi Motup
One of the best buddies of Colonel Chhewang Rinchen

Colonel Thakur Prithi Chand, MVC of 2 Dogra

Subedar Bhim Chand,
VrC & Bar of 2 Dogra

General Jayanto Nath Choudhury,
OBE, the then COAS Pinning
The Sena Medal to
Lieutenant Chhewang Rinchen

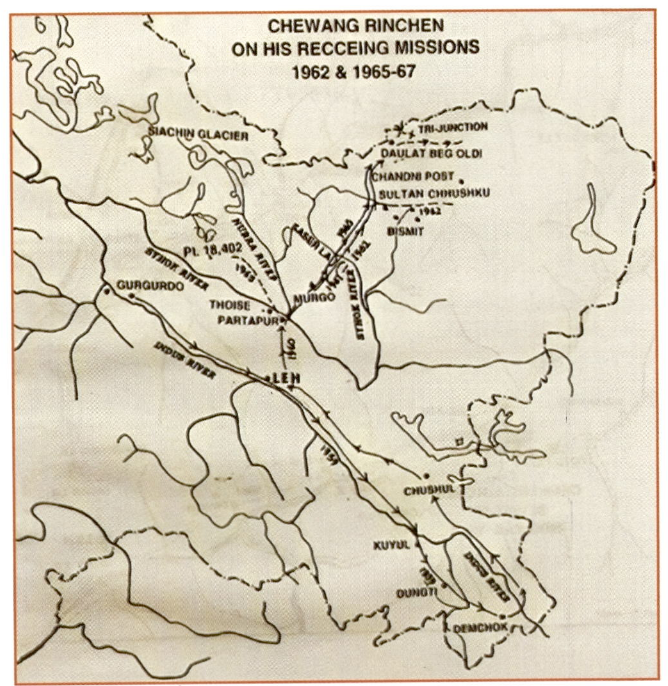

Brigadier T.B. Kapoor, AVSM Sector Commander of Partapur (Mid 1965 – 1967)

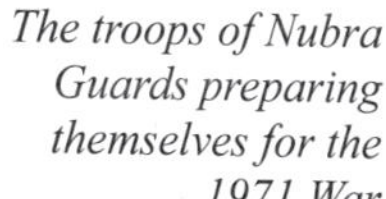

The troops of Nubra Guards preparing themselves for the 1971 War

Major Chhewang Rinchen, MVC & SM, addressing his troops of Ladakh Scouts & Nubra Guards before the beginning of the Operations for 1971 War

Lieutenant General Sartaj Singh, George Medal & Padma Bhushan Corps Commander of 15 Corps during 1971 War

Lieutenant General S.P. Malhotra, Padma Bhushan, PVSM GOC 3 Infantry Division during 1971 war & Former Commandant of DSSC Wellington (1972-75)

Major Chhewang Rinchen, MVC & SM, Addressing the locals of Turtuk after the Victory of Turtuk in 1971 War

Shri Varahagiri Venkata Giri, the then President of India, Pinning The Second Mahavir Chakra to Major Chhewang Rinchen

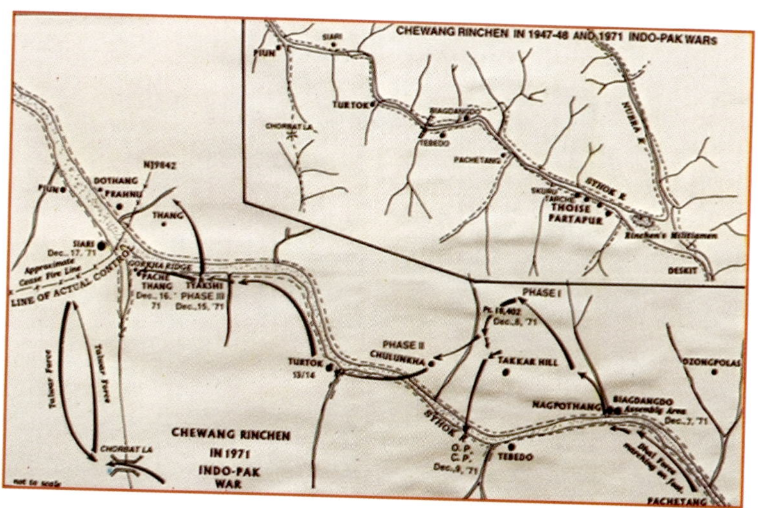

Lieutenant Colonel (then Captain) Shashi Anand, Adjutant of Ladakh Scouts during 1971 war

Colonel Chhewang Rinchen with his third daughter Tina at Khardung La

Colonel Chhewang Rinchen with a Young Lieutenant of his unit

Colonel Chhewang Rinchen with his buddies of Ladakh Scouts

Colonel Chhewang Rinchen with his family in New Delhi

Colonel Chhewang Rinchen during the Regimental gatherings

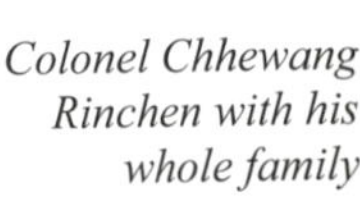

Colonel Chhewang Rinchen with his whole family

General Arun Sridhar Vaidya, MVC & Bar, the then COAS, Congratulating Major Chhewang Rinchen, MVC & Bar, SM on promotion to Lieutenant Colonel Rank

Colonel Chhewang Rinchen with the villagers

Colonel Chhewang Rinchen with his counterpart from the Indian Air Force

Colonel Chhewang Rinchen with his Holiness Dalai Lama

Shri Raj Nath Singh, the Defense Minister of India, inaugurating India's highest altitude all-weather permanent bridge, ***The Chhewang Rinchen Setu***

Chapter 8

Myth Behind the Peace

The unorganised stones had cohesive tales of history to narrate, freezing herbs and flowing silent wave of wind with visuals of lush greenery between the oasis of snowy hills had been passing the days with expectation of tranquillity. The explicate view of the region had a baffling visual of godly mountains of the Himalayas. The nature rationally allowing a plethora of soothing scenery chided the hearts and minds. This was the peripheral axis of the Nubra Valley at the western frontier acting as an arm of northern Ladakh adjoining Baltistan which is, now, under the bleeding claws of enemies.

Resonance of the 16-year-old war was about to knock as Shockwave in a new form.

The Valley of Flowers was in the stoic silence after Dragon's claw failed to grip over the valley in the 1962 war for the three years.

In mid-1965, a covert flare up was taking place in the northwestern frontier of Nubra Valley. In the wake of any response by the enemies from the critical vantage point of passage adjoining Baltistan under the feet of Karakoram heights. The region was Northern Ladakh and the same engraved point of the 1948 War's Incineration. In Indian military administrative chronology, the region northern Ladakh was hailed as Partapur Sector. It was under the watch of Colonel T.B. Kapur in 1965. The long moustache man with vibrant eyes on the sight was one of the best commanders to be put onto the spot in that critical sector. He was the man with full preparedness to meet any misadventure of hostile elements. Just down towards the south of Nubra, the vanguard of the Kargil Sector existed and it had been under constant threat by the Pakistani forces from the Chorbat axis.

To gain a strategic edge over regional boundaries against the adversaries, Col. Kapur pressed the high command for permission to grasp Turtuk/Chorbat territory within the control of the Indian Army from the North to neutralise the enemy's ability to stress the left flank resulting to ease the Kargil front for guarding. After endless efforts to convince superiors, Col. Kapur's plan to capture Turtuk/Chorbat was given a green signal but soon when the Commander requested additional forces to carry out the attack, higher authorities put a halt to this brilliant mission due to disagreement over the deployment of additional troops.

The decision came as a temporary hex for the Commander. Discarding such a potential mission would have been a large disadvantage according to his experience but it took no time for him to stand again with his wit and determination to go ahead with the different orders available in the operative paradigm.

On 12 May 1965, Col. Kapur sought the permission of the Higher Headquarters to carry out limited operations on the Baltistan front with his available force only and it was made clear that no additional troops would be made available for this operation.

Expediently hc agreed to the orders like it seemed he had a complete idea about how to execute the mission. Later he was conveyed that a force of about 2000 enemy infiltrators was advancing, towards his sector on the Ladakh range from Chorbat La to cut off his sector from the rest of Ladakh. Col. Kapur soon realised the golden window which made itself available.

The Black Rock fort which was once the helm of the Indian Army, after the 1948 war, was given to Pakistani forces due to the ceasefire line agreement. Talking about the place's credibility, it acted as the centrepiece of the region to establish the eyes over the land downwards to the Nubra Valley from the western front and as a vantage point against Baltistan. This fact alone underlined the significance of the fort and it dashed up in the form of optimistic thoughts in the Colonel's mind.

The spark of realisation to recapture the Black Rock fort, Colonel Kapur started to design his intent of action and shifted his tactical headquarters from Partapur to Baigdangdo. His watch began on May 13, 1965, for three days, he kept monitoring the enemy's activities in the Black Rock area. This was all about building the viable course of the plan for the mission to capture the fort.

By the third day, he constructed an entire picture of the scenario and orchestrated an assured plan for the operation. A piece of crucial information knocked on the desk of the Colonel in which he discovered the loophole in the patrolling regime of the enemy which later turned into a robust opportunity of a window to surprise them.

The enemy troops used to arrive regularly to occupy the position by 0500 hours and vacated it at nightfall. Seeing this kind of patrolling, one thing was sure. The enemy was unable to operate in the devilish cold of the night when the temperature drops drastically below zero degrees Celsius, the reason they needed to return to a safer and warm position. It made one more thing clear. The enemy will not expect a surprise attack on the post, giving crucial leverage for the mission.

This information of the enemy patrolling schedule was confirmed by the locals who also informed the Commander that it had been going on for the past 15/16 years since the day the fort was given to Pakistani forces by the effect of the UN Ceasefire Agreement. Finally, Colonel Kapur decided to launch a covert attack on the night of May 17/18, 1965. Captain Amrik Singh Gill of the newly formed Ladakh Scouts was assigned this job. Ladakh Scouts were made with unifying the reckoning forces of two Militia (Ladakhi) Battalions. This unit was specially created for mountain and guerrilla warfare due to its need in baffling warfare in the laps of these treacherous summits.

Capt. Gill was given liberty to build his force for the operation; the strength of the force was decided up to 150 jawans from the troops deployed in Nubra. All soldiers in the sector were no less than flaming lanterns of willpower and skill, in a way these men were known to hunt in snow stealthily. Capt. Gill carried out his simulation and practice of operation in the neighbouring area for two days. On the day of operation Captain and his force captured the empty fort at the scheduled date, waiting for enemies with the spear stroking and claw nailing style of attacking plan.

The next morning brave leopards of the Indian Army were waiting for their prey, with complete awareness to give a blazing welcome to the enemy forces which, as usual, were coming to reoccupy the Black Rock as per their 16-year-old foolish schedule. As the enemy forces were close as 150 metres from the newly occupied Indian post, Captain Amrik Singh Gill signalled his Nubran jawans to rein hell over Pakistanis with a brutal wave of attack. The enemy forces were psychologically unprepared to fathom such a large-scale attack; this led them to run for their lives leaving their arms and ammunition, rations, and bedding. The entire operation was over in less than three hours and the Indian Army took control over the Black Rock fort successfully.

As soon as the news of Black Rock fort capturing spread in local villages, the Nubrans ushered in jubilant smiles and giggles. They were very happy with this victory of the Indian Army and this success was a boon of the moment to them since it gave them almost 250 sq.km of the area as grazing ground for their animals which had been denied to them unfairly for the past 16 years. For the next 2 months, the Indian Army consolidated and reinforced its position on that Karakoram Pass and Shyok river bends at the northernmost part of the Chorbat axis. Also, the trijunction needed a strong force of sentinels to amplify the magnitude of grip over those critical passes especially the region between Saser La, Partapur and the DBO sector which are geographically the three strategic points of India's northernmost frontier which acted as a triad of vantage points to monitor the movements of Pakistani and Chinese hostile elements.

Two months later, in the vicinity of Daulat Beg Oldi in July 1965, the surreal gaze of white cloak could be felt on the trenches of meticulous steeps at a height of 4,570 metres. This was the north-eastern frontier where the Tiger of Ladakh is on watch.

"Nonnos, just one more match and let's see who will win." The vibrant voice of the Tiger pitched up from an adjacent playground made by jawans deployed on the post. The ground was made with stones keeping in a rectangular shape to create a perimeter of the playground and a line of cans was used to partition from the middle.

Our leopards were playing volleyball with the Tiger. Chhewang Rinchen, now a Captain attached to the Ladakh Scouts, was posted in the Northern region of Daulat Beg Oldi sector on the Indo-Chinese border. During dawn, while Capt. Rinchen was playing volleyball, a runner came to him with a wireless message which read 'Personal from Tiger Delta Sector to Tiger DBO, Report to the headquarters immediately, Hand over the command to Lamb (Second-in-Command).' After listening to those orders, Rinchen stepped towards the post, summoned his Second-in-Command and relieved himself from the Commanding post. The Tiger was obedient with sparkling pride as he wasted no time and got ready with his bedding rolled up. Rinchen left his headquarters for the Sector Headquarters early at 4 am the next morning. He took a small escort party, a few mules, and his riding pony. He galloped at breakneck speed and covered the distance of about ten days' normal march in just five days. In the span of 17 years of his service over this untenable land with precarious cold winds, Rinchen has seen many ruthless times bluntly. It was another day in the office for him travelling in such unfavourable conditions and reaching before time. No wonder he was an impenetrable fortress of entrenched willpower.

Before arriving at Sector HQ, Rinchen had one day stop at his home in Sumur. The exuberant eyes of his parents, wife, and children made his brutal journey worthy. He spent quality time with his loved ones and left the other day without fail.

After he arrived at HQ, he met Colonel Kapur for the first time. This was no less than an epic moment when Rinchen met someone who matched his frequency of personality. Rinchen developed a great love and high respect for him like a student develops for his Guru on the very first meeting. Col. Kapur had a proactive approach with whoever he meets and it was well-matched from his look of six feet tall with fearsome Pathan moustaches, he was a rare combination of soldierly qualities and exceptionally gutful and high-spirited nature.

He shined like a foremost idol of treasured experience in combat. During the briefing the Colonel gave Capt. Rinchen a very warm handshake and, patting him on his back, he said, "My brave Tiger of Nubra, I am happy to see you arrive so fast. How the hell could you manage to reach Partapur so early?"

Rinchen misunderstood what the Colonel said and thought that he was being sarcastic and expected him to have arrived much earlier. As a simple soldier, Rinchen started explaining his position promptly, "For five days and five nights, I have been travelling at a breakneck speed to arrive at Partapur. My only stop was at Sumur, my hometown so that I could see the members of my family, meet my old parents and children, and have a hot meal." Listening to Rinchen's explanation, Colonel understood the straightforward nature and simplicity Rinchen possessed; these few qualities of Rinchen convinced Colonel about him.

The same evening, he was briefed by the Colonel for the special task for which he had been called from the Daulat Beg Oldi sector. Rinchen realised soon where he will be needed this time. He was familiar with this region and had a ferocious reputation to operate on the western front. Rinchen came to know by his staff officers at the Headquarters that only a few days back at the end of a meeting, the Colonel had ordered his Brigade Major to get him the best 'Snow Tiger' for a very special task he had in mind. Many names of brave and dashing officers of Ladakh Scouts were placed before him but, finally, the old man said, "I want, Rinchen the Tiger of Nubra for this special task." Rinchen had the sheer capability of being a dauntless warrior to operate in these inhospitable terrains. He was more than a soldier and adhered to all qualities of a predator and with all acceptable stands; he was the alpha of his unit too.

Rinchen had a reputation in all the northern commands as an excellent mountain soldier. This statement was proven by his ability to travel fast and reach before time. Despite having hardships in the journey, he knew every inch of soil and snow of the region even after assuming charge of DBO as new Station Commander. Rinchen's brainchild and one of the founding stones of Ladakh Scouts were still functioning independently in the required region of Ladakh even after becoming a major and inseparable component of Ladakh Scouts. Under the leadership of Colonel Kapur, Rinchen saw the potential to grow his unit into a larger and formidable force at a respectable strength. Captain Rinchen had the satisfaction of serving under Colonel Kapur to the best of his capacity since the first day. Captain Rinchen was entrusted with three very important tasks. His orders were to raise the Nubra Guards of 1000 strong as a voluntary force which was to be armed with. 303mm calibre assault rifles. With this force, he was ordered to carry out deep penetration patrolling in the eastern side of the Baigdangdo Sector and to check the infiltration into the Ladakh range and also to threaten the Sabz Kot cliff overlooking the Shyok River bend on the enemy side of Baltistan. Furthermore, he needed to carry out reconnaissance in force on the western side of the Black Rock Fort which was constantly under pressure ever since it had been captured. Colonel Kapur needed every bit of untainted information beyond the perimeter to understand the movement of enemies.

The Commander had made up his mind to attack Chulunkha and Turtuk from the northwest. The prominence of these sectors was hugely important to establish a ranging advantage over the enemies. The colonel knew that the Black Rock fort could be a stepping stone to acquire these positions which are inside the enemy's belly. And the Colonel wanted to rip that belly and bring Turtuk in the lap of Indian sovereignty. It is now a necessity for Captain Chhewang Rinchen, the Tiger of Nubra, to assume his role in this operation. Rinchen completed his preliminary tasks and submitted his full report to the Commander about the reconnaissance he had made on the western side of Baigdangdo and the information he had gathered about the infiltrators on the Ladakh range.

During the reconnaissance, Rinchen made sure the enemy would be cornered and the pressure on Sabz Kot should disappear; later, this performance resulted in the withdrawal of enemy forces. Identifying the window of attack, Rinchen initiated an attack on Sabz Kot under orders of his Commander, thus capturing that important side of the boundary.

This perfect execution of the plan brought Sabz Kot under the Indian Army control but the Colonel didn't decide to stop here. He had an altogether different idea to stomp in action. On August 25, 1965, Rinchen was again summoned by the Commander for a fresh briefing on the northwestern side. The Commander was very clear regarding his plans of attack and, hence, the urgency.

Rinchen was required to go on recon to extract the information regarding the strength of the enemy troops on each post. The type of weapons in service with enemies and their supply chain route. Rinchen saluted his Commander after receiving orders and gathered his required team including his junior NCO Havaldar P. Stobdan and his chosen few who excelled in mountain climbing. For Rinchen, Havaldar P. Stobdan was like his aide on mountain journeys in that part of the sector; he was like an ibex in the mountains. Such gutted down survival skill made the Nubrans, the spear tip of mountain warfare. After collecting his men for the task, he left.

Rinchen was out for a week to collect information and to extract the intelligence He climbed up the highest range point at a height of 5,610 metres and then he rolled down to the rear of the enemy positions. During his childhood, Rinchen had this thrilling habit of climbing hilltops and rolling down, he never expected his curiosity of mountain climbing would become his strength deep down into his soldiering qualities.

By August 1965, below the neck of Nubra Valley at Haji Peer and Kargil region Pakistani leadership made a big mistake in the wake of desperation to invade Kashmir. Pakistan inserted their guerrilla infiltrators into Kashmir under Operation Gibraltar, these infiltrators were the Mujahideen and Razakars. They were divided into 10 Divisions under regular army commanders. These forces began to push inside Indian borders like a directionless march past. Pak forces were convinced of an illusion by their leaders that Kashmiris were unhappy with Indian Rule; they failed to recognise the wave perception flowing in Indian administered Kashmir. Two groups of Gibraltar forces crossed the line of ceasefire and entered India in the hope of getting a massive swirl of support from Kashmiri Muslims.

On 9th August 1965, about 100 infiltrators attacked Poonch for several days. India finally broke its silence and launched a counteroffensive attack with heavy firepower and defeated them.

This infiltration was confirmed by the U.N. Military Observer in India and Pakistan. India was left with no option but to change the gear into brutal offensive operations beyond the line. On 15 August 1965, the Indian Army occupied the Pakistan position at Kargil and the Haji Pir pass. This action by India completely halted the Pakistani movement, blowing them into crumbles of surrendered chunks. In the Punjab sector, the Indian Army reached Lahore, putting Pakistan into a nightmare that day. Operation Gibraltar terribly failed. All over the ceasefire line, conflicts started except the Nubra Valley and Karakoram Pass where Rinchen under Col. Kapur was laying the formidable blow against the Turtuk complex.

Reaching the vantage point at the rear of the enemy line Rinchen and Co. Started their intelligence gathering and began monitoring the passes and keeping a strict vigil over movements, Rinchen ordered his men to keep an eye on all critical points of the enemy position and he alone jumped in those enemy lines like a stealthy leopard in the silent snowy night to collect the information. Further Capt. Rinchen was ordered to forge ahead at the Baigdangdo subsector and measure the exact strength of the enemy personnel and position of the Pak forces deployed in the area. He was also required to locate an approach for any offensive operation if the scenario demands that option. Rinchen was prepared for any outcome.

Rinchen was given a task force involving two small groups of recon and protection units. He planned to reconnaissance from two different patrolling approaches. Rinchen devised a plan to mark all high passes in that sector to understand the navigational routes of the enemy. Each time during his patrol NCO P. Stobdan was ordered to secure a 'La' in Ladakhi dialect. "La" means "passes", with this order Rinchen notified his recon unit to keep strict vigilance under the NCO. With the second recon unit, Chhewang Rinchen reached the peak of the mountain at a height of 5,610 metres. Since Ladakh and its surroundings were the critical landmasses of high mountainous passes, climbing such peaks were a habit for Nubrans. Such a vantage point has all along been of great tactical importance in the sense that it can act as the most commanding observation post for both Pakistan and India. From this point, one could have a clear view of the entire Nubra Valley including the Indian Sector Headquarters, roads and bridges and the airfield and, also, the Sector Headquarters, roads and bridges, disposition of installations and approaches right up to Chorbat La on the Pakistan side. For this reason, the ceasefire line of 1 January 1949, had been drawn through that point. It was literally a high-altitude sentinel's standpoint to watch at such a high degree of region increasing the envelope of visual range drastically.

After concentrating on the passes which were marked by the first patrol unit, Rinchen found the fine traces on the snow and empty tins lying all around indicating clearly that the Pakistanis had patrolled that area just before a few moments of course. After a thorough observation of the ground and disposition of Pakistan troops, Rinchen reported to the Commander that a wing minus a company was the strength of the Pakistanis in the Nubra sector. The numbers of footmarks and a precise hunch about the waste tin around the region confirmed him at accuracy.

The Commander was amazed by Rinchen's analysis. He took an immediate decision to launch an offensive mission to capture Chulunkha and Turtuk. His spirit was sky high and his plan was laying full proof on-ground scenario but the higher authorities did not permit him to do so and advised him to be satisfied with a strong defence against any possible offensive action by the Pakistanis. The higher officials' coherence into such a defensive strategy was a kind of Achilles heel. This peaceful posture of leadership was an unfair peril of patience for soldiers.

By 1st September 1965, when Operation Gibralter was slammed hard in mud, Pakistan launched a counterattack, called Operation Grand Slam, with the mission to capture Akhnoor in Jammu which was like a signal junction for the Indian Army.

Capturing it would mean communications cut off and destroying supply routes to Indian troops. Pakistani General Ayub Khan spoke an infamous word during the attack - "Hindu morale would not stand more than a couple of hard blows at the right time and place". He underestimated the might of the Indian Army on that day which later came to realisation when the Grand Slam turned into grand mockery for Pakistani forces. Indian troops were surprised by the attack on Akhnoor. Pak expected the arrival of the Indian Air Force and soon the ground warfare turned into Air Warfare after Pak Air Force came to rescue their dolls. Seeing this kind of unprecedented conflict, the Indian Army did the unthinkable and opened a war theatre at the Punjab front, exposing Lahore in distress. In sheer panic, Pakistan diverted its forces towards Punjab and further south leaving Kargil front defenceless where Pak Army had high peaks in control at the western edge of Kargil, despite Kargil being under Indian administration. In futile desperation to invade Kashmir, Pakistan clearly lost the edge at all war theatre. Even in Rajasthan, Pakistani tank regiments were thrashed up in heavy tank fights, rendering Pak Patton tanks into dust.

Between kinetic actions in South Kashmir, the edges of the northern region were still silent on September 15, when the entire plethora of northern command was busy at southern Kashmir from Kargil. Both Tigers of Baigdangdo Sector were standing at the edge of Nubra, completing all preparations for the final assault on the Turtuk complex. Only the assault day was waiting. The Commander was waiting for the full moon. Besides, there was the fear of a coalition of China with Pakistan, a threat to the same effect having been issued by China to India. Ultimately, the higher authorities decided not to permit Colonel Kapur to carry out his grand design. This literally broke the heart of that confident Commander with the rest of his force who were ready to blow the enemy with a wave of attack. Rinchen was also saddened but he took time to measure the depth of dissatisfaction Col. Kapur had on that event.

Accepting the decision simultaneously, Rinchen diverted his focus on the task of recruiting more Nubrans young blood to the Nubra Guards to raise its strength to a thousand as directed by the Station Commander. It was not only the number that mattered; they had to be well-trained in the use of infantry arms and successfully core them into soldier's form. Since 1948, a sizeable proportion of the Valley's population had remained militarily trained to meet any emergent challenge from across the borders; which later motivated youngsters to join the Army, seeing Rinchen as a role model. To support the cause, the entire strength of the Nubra Guards and the personnel of the Indian Army had been supplied free rations by the locals during the 1948 war for several months. It substantially put the entire community of Nubra in a respectable position of value for the Indian Army.

Rinchen was still overseeing the training apart from continuously rolling to the recon missions, from head to toe all effort poured in to train the youngsters of the Nubra in the very best way in warfare drill, usage of military assets and the use of weapons. Under the voice of Rinchen, every blunt soul in force slowly turned into a sharp soldier hinting at the Nubrans' nature being eligible for a military career. By the first dawn of September 1965, the Nubra Guards had been transformed into the Ladakh Scouts and dissolved their composition completely within the brand-new Ladakh Scouts. The scouts became an integral part of the Indian Army. The Nubrans are called children of the mountain for a reason, naturally, they were keen on surviving in such high ranges and that feature was singularly polished to turn them into highly mobile units and allow them to master the tactics of mountain and guerrilla warfare. The blazing force of Ladakh scouts was ready.

The ranges of conflicts that erupted across the ceasefire line pushed the Indian Army to cross the international border on the 8th of September, 1965 as Indian forces attacked areas all along the western borders from Pathankot to Lahore and captured a large region of Lahore. Seeing such escalations day by day, Colonel Kapur, remaining ever prepared for any emergency, entrusted Chhewang Rinchen with the responsibility of affecting liaison with the local leaders for any possible emergent engagement.

Since being the face of Nubra Valley on behalf of the Indian Army, any soul in Ladakh would have followed Rinchen without question. His words were honoured in all region. Col. Kapur asked Capt. Rinchen who was Commander of the Nubra Guards to keep his volunteers alert and make themselves available at the shortest possible notice for the front. The potential action which Rinchen was expecting needed a good supply of ammunition too. The Nubra Guards, realising this, asked for more arms and ammunition as the number of volunteers was expected to be considerably larger than the count. Rinchen put up a suggestion before the Commander to increase the strength of the Nubra Guards to one battalion which the Commander readily agreed to and the requirement of arms was met with adequately. In August 1965, the entire force was ready to lead the assault on the first signal from their Commander. And each one of the soldiers was waiting for that command.

Ladakh is known as the “Land of high passes”, and had its own problem for people living there and it verily brought a critical hurdle for the Nubra Guards. The hurdle was a lack of suitable means of transport and communication between Leh and the Nubra Valley where any confrontation against the Pakistanis was likely to take place. The region was indeed treacherous one to travel Since the locals were adapted well to these harsh terrains, yet the region was not suited well for large mobilisation of forces, the only access to the Nubra Valley was across the Khardung La. The Nubra-Leh road via Khardung La was still under construction and was not yet open to traffic. It took four days from Leh to reach the Battalion Headquarters at Baigdangdo. The Indian Army units in the region would suffer from the great handicap in matters of adequate and timely logistic support if any worthwhile offensive operations were to be undertaken in that area. It turned out to be a great peril for the northern command, especially for the posted units. The ghost of the 1962 war was enough to haunt about the same mistake, the lack of transportation and necessary roads indeed was the fruit of negligence about that land.

The air service from Leh or Pathankot was utilised for airdropping of essential resources but that was also not enough, the basics necessities like rations, fodder, and ammunition were transported on great efforts, but it was not enough in the wake of sudden assault from the enemy. A healthy chain of supply was the need of the hour. Quick reinforcements for any offensive venture or even a strong defence for that matter, the means of transportation was turning into weakness in the region for the Army. By mid of September when conflicts manifested into a complete out blown war on the border, the air flights to Nubra had to be stopped and, as a result, no mail arrived, nor did any fresh supplies. Leaving Khardung La pass only emphasised routes for essential supplies and mail, which were continued to be received by the land routes across the Khardung La. The only means of communication with Leh was by wireless and the radio. The wireless could hardly enable the people to know what exactly was happening elsewhere across the ceasefire line. It was only through the radio that they learnt that Kargil had been in the thick of a fierce battle. The weak means of communication and single enforced route for supplies put Ladakh Scouts on the back front of action for a greater period. The scenery at Baigdangdo and Partapur frontier was still silent compared to what was happening below Kargil.

Whereas the Kargil front and Haji Peer pass were flaring up, the Baigdangdo and Partapur Sector were Numb in cold. After Colonel Kapur, the Sector Commander at Partapur was denied permission to launch an attack on the Pakistani post at Chulunkha Turtuk complex. He looked out to keep the defences strong in that direction and for a time being, he extinguished the flame of his intent to capture Turtuk. His superiors warned him to ensure that the Daulat Beg Oldi Trijunction sector was duly reinforced at the earliest, fearing the Chinese misadventure on all three sides. HQ updated the Commander about diversionary grilling acts by the Chinese. As there were cases of minor firing on the north and north-east borders, it became compulsory to ensure reinforcement of the DBO Trijunction sector immediately. Practically on the measuring scale, Karakoram Pass and DBO are not farther from each other, and due to such boundary circumstances, the Trijunction turned to be a more critical sector to safeguard.

The Indian Army was prepared well to tackle surprise attacks by Pak forces but it would have been very risky to take any chances with the Chinese especially at the DBO front, particularly given the security treaty signed by Pakistan and China in March 1963. The treaty enclaves about Chinese aid to Pakistan in dire need, Indian Leaders were quite aware of that, even since being the forefront banner raiser of Non-Aligned Movement, the Indian Government knew the importance of help by friendly nations. Back at Partapur base, Capt. Rinchen was ordered to move back to the Trijunction area on the Karakoram Range and join his former unit. Col. Kapur was ordered to move his operating core from Partapur to DBO Trijunction and beautifully the Commander of the force joined his men to such dreaded long march, it was heartening for his troops to see the Commander also move along with his force, with him entire tactical headquarters were also moved.

From Baltistan to Karakoram, if they took a common route then it would have been a fortnight of hellish march. Rinchen knew this problem and Col. Kapur was ordered to reach Trijunction by 28th September. A strict but brutal approach was needed during the move with high morale, the troops needed to cross the river junction of Nubra and Shyok flowing. Despite the defiance of the flow of the river and the drab landscape of a snow blanket, it failed to reduce the boldness of the soldiers to cross it. Troops were required to cross the river junction at Thulumputi but there were no bridges across the rivers and they had to swim across, which was not only difficult but very risky, yet it was not enough to stop Rinchen's men to halt there. Rinchen knew that the risk had to be taken because the obligation to move forces within the time frame was necessary, and delays were not acceptable to the Tiger.

Like a beast of survival, Rinchen took every muscle power of his men for making rafts and rope bridges. Shivering through the entire night they crafted the means of crossing the river. By the morning of 20th September, Rinchen's forces started crossing the rivers. By 1500 hours, the forces had got across and were ready to move to Saser La, the continuous moving of Shaktiman trucks led by two stallions, ridden by Capt. Rinchen and Col. Kapur were shaking the passage route in rumble as they moved ahead in night. Every "La" of Ladakh knew these children of the mountain led by the Tiger.

Trailblazing movement of troops and Rinchen's leading ability was not just an eye candy for Commander but also an incredible sight, Col. Kapur was exceedingly happy with the progress. The day's sweating effort by all men was pretty exhausting to each one of them. Seeing this Col. Kapur ordered the forces to rest on the home side of Saser-Brangsa Pass for three hours and have tea and food. At midnight of 300 hours, the crossing of the Saser Pass commenced. By 600 hours at the first light of the day, the forces reached Saser post after crossing the Pass in just a count of 3 hours at the helm of the bright day.

Such intense and quick mobilisation of force with conspicuous breath and indispensable motif was unreal to the eyes but these leopards actually made it with flawless determination. Rinchen was satisfied with his troops and he credited it to the presence of their Commander whom Rinchen begin to see as the source of great inspiration to his leopards who made it to the Trijunction, Saser Braganza Pass has a reputation to be the roughest and cruellest passage in the Himalayas, nevertheless like a Gates of Inferno the Pass was. Never in the history of Saser-Brangsa Pass, had any force ever crossed that ruthless and dreaded callous passage in such massive strength so blisteringly quick. The moving of troops and every actionable event were noted down by the Commander in his recording notes. The forces arrived at the position by the evening of 25 September, 3 days ahead of the given deadline. The Saser La journey was completed in mere 4 days, whereas it would have been 15 long days from the common route. The impossible task was executed here beautifully.

As high passes of Karakoram witnessed the bold mobilisation of Nubra guards, the fickle tool of geopolitics has landed 751 kms away in the capital of the country. UNSC passed a unanimous resolution to stop the advancement of conflicts on the border by both sides within 48 hours and demanded a ceasefire at an immediate effect 5 days earlier on 20th September. India accepted the decision at the very same moment. By that time, Indian forces were already holding the upper hand at all war threats against Pak forces, Pak president Ayub Khan took 3 days to accept the resolution since Pakistan failed to gain any leverage from this war, not even any support from the international stage. This war was a strategic and political defeat of Pakistan at the cost of their dwindling economic growth which drastically slowed down after the war.

A great number of troops belonging to glorious and diverse regiments participated in these chronicles. With the hot zone of sieges and flickering number of skirmishes, the 1965 war saw both types of dynamic actions. Witness of the greatest valiant and intrepid tales also took place in this phase of the war, as one of greatest tank warfare was witnessed in the battle of Assal Uttar, the most celebrated victory of 1965 on 11 September executed by forces of Deccan Horse. 3 Cavalry, 91 Mountain

Regiment, 40 Medium Regiment, 4 Grenadiers, 18 Rajputana Rifles, 1 Dogra, 2 Mahar, and 9 JAK RIF armed with Centurion, Sherman and AMX-13 tanks against the double size of force composed of Patton tanks by Pakistani forces. Battle took notice of every eye in the world and there is some unsung battle fought silently in blizzarding northern mountains by a unit which was least known once upon an era. The newly created Ladakh Scouts did the unthinkable.

Superiors in Headquarters came to surprise after listening to the update about Ladakh Scouts presence on battle positions in the Trijunction with their Commander at a direct charge of operations on the spot successfully before the given ultimatum. Chinese eyes were on the Indian border since day 1 of the war, the silence they kept all along was a clear signal that China was cautious to do any misadventure. The Chinese Army understood that the Indian Army was not the same as it was in 1962. The very presence of a section of armed Indian troops that too specialised in mountain warfare at the Trijunction became a symbol of India's might to its zenith. It was a warning to both China and Pakistan; China might not be able to corner India again after the 1962 Sham. Meanwhile, Pakistan also realised the inability of the Chinese Treaty despite all pledges made to aid, China took zero effort to provide material help to Pakistan and could not go beyond 'moral support'. Both Pakistan and China failed to throw India off-balance, resulting in China being silent on-ground and humiliating defeat of Pakistan on both the battlefield and the geopolitical arena.

It took years to instill rightful attention to the Ladakh Scouts. There were many battles, for instance, where the great valour of some units went unnoticed or shadowed under course of events, which didn't have the way to reach the recorded history due to unfortunate circumstances. An obvious example of such a scenario was witnessed in the same year in the Battle of Dograi. The famed and audacious siege by the Indian Army units that the task was to capture a town inside the enemy's line, deeply eight kms from our land was a gallant ode to be told. The Feisty and glaring action in mid-September on the Dograi front led to earn countless gallantry awards and battle honour to the brave 3 JAT led by Lt. Col. Desmond Hayde, who earned MVC himself; the platoon was in operation to capture Dograi in early September. For masses, it was believed to be a single unit effort for the fall of Dograi, but the reality resonated with the different picture and narration. The 3 JAT was not alone in this glorious assault; the endeavour of 3 JAT was assisted by the 13 Punjab Battalion also known as JIND Infantry, the 54th Infantry Brigade, the 15th Infantry Division, the 14 Horse, the 15 Dogra, and a smaller number of troops from the 7 Punjab with Artillery support from the 60th Heavy Artillery Regiment.

Since the start of the operation on this front, grip over Dograi was getting delayed due to miscommunication with the other units until the arrival of 13 Punjab (JIND) were in operation to capture rail bridges and enemy posts of icchogil canal since deployment and continued to attack east bank of river with 15 Infantry Division. Addition to it, 13 Punjab (JIND) contributed in action to cut off communication lines between Lahore and Wagha, the troops were in movement since the first week of September. All forces devised the plan to thwart enemies and push them back from the region to capture the Dograi leading to Lahore, leaving them no position to gain advantage ahead of Dograi, by the time of circling canals on the east bank, 13 Punjab (JIND) was commanded by Lt.Col M Chaterjee until Lt.Col EDH Nanavati took over the charge of Battalion at 12th September 1965. The precursor action for the main battle continued to progress for days through the combined efforts from 3 JAT, the 13 Punjab (JIND), the 54th Infantry Brigade, and other assisting units. Brigadier Niranjan Singh,MC, was leading the 54th Infantry Brigade.

Lt. Col. Hayde had all available resources to plan a phasewise assault bringing Pakistani troops of the 16 Punjab, the 8 Punjab, the 3 Baluch, and the 18 Baluch forces composed of more than 1000 strong forces onto their knees in front of 550+ men of the Indian Army. The Dograi siege was a fascinating battle. The attack on Dograi required a spearhead assault before the large-scale attack by the 3 JAT and other units, the 13 Punjab (JIND) and the 54th Infantry Brigade were meant to be the tip of the spear in this mission.

The strategy to capture Dograi was based on two phases; the 13 Punjab (JIND) and the 54th Infantry Brigade were assigned to spearhead the operation on the first phase where the 13 Punjab (JIND) will storm Mile 13 Area and Canal defence would be under a combined attack by the 54th Infantry Brigade with other units like the 7 Punjab. The first phase of assault was a dynamic attempt to break the enemy spine on their positions at the east bank canal adjacent to Grand Trunk Road leading inside the Dograi. The success meant obliterating Pakistan's last stronghold on the GT Road, ending the reinforcement and leaving them defenceless deep within. Later, during the final wave of assault in the second phase, which was decided to be a boundless strike at a wide flank, the 3 JAT was in the position to execute it.

Ichhogil canal was already captured during the first week of September but due to delay in providing additional troops and stiffs of massive reinforcement by the 16 Punjab of Pakistan Army, the 3 JAT had to retreat; but before the withdraw, Lt.Col. Hayde Proved his mettle on the Batapore front successfully. After the arrival of the additional troops, the final plan was laid to destroy Dograi front once and for all. Immediately after a few days, the 13 Punjab (JIND) kept aggressive standing with the 15 Dogra and the 3 JAT, while the 7th Infantry Division also assisted in endeavour to lay advancing on Icchogil canal after Barki campaign, the enemy sector itself had considerable defence potential for counterattack and shielded Lahore from Indian offensive thrusts.

The mission began at dawn of 21st September 1965. Midnight period of 21-22 September was chosen for launching the assault. As per the proposed plan, the 13 Punjab (JIND) stormed heavily guarded Mile 13 area, they faced heavy rain of fire halting their speed for a while, wasting no time, The 13 Punjab (JIND) reattempted the assault again dauntlessly and this time success bowed leading them to Capture Mile 13 area, the Commanding Officer of 13 Punjab (JIND) personally led the assault with 75 personnel, JCOs and ORs. On another side, the 54th Infantry Brigade with the 15 Dogra and the 15th Infantry Division breached the canal defence, giving Lt. Col. Hayde his golden chance to blizzard the enemy post deep inside town that were unaware of the recent defeat of their fellow units. One of the fierce and intensely bloody battles took place in Dograi. The 3 JAT led the advance at night and destroyed the enemy's last flank in the course of 27 hours of battle, leading the Pakistani Army to have casualties of more than 300 soldiers. The 13 Punjab (JIND) had their share of success with capturing numerous enemy assets, including four Sherman tanks, six recoilless gun systems, and eight jeeps, with a countless number of ammunitions.

After the execution of a well-devised plan and capturing Dograi, a ceasefire was declared. The 3 JAT were honoured with numerous accolades for their heroic service, which they truly deserved. Some units got Battle and Theatre honours including the 13 Punjab (JIND), 14Horse and the 54th Infantry Brigade, however somewhere in these upscale events, the efforts of 13 Punjab (JIND), the 54th Infantry Brigade and the 15th Infantry Division with other unit's contributions, unfortunately got unnoticed by history in tides of time. Yet a unit will serve, and their men will be ready to fight at the moment they are summoned on battle frontiers. The storming of Mile 13 and Ichhogil Canal in Dograi siege was a fascinating battle of rare grit- resilient officers and fearless troops displayed deathless heroism against a superior in number and well-prepared enemy to capture critical posts like mile 13. History does not record too many instances when an Infantry Battalion undertook a frontal attack with these challenges; without adequate information or maps and with a depleted strength lost in previous skirmishes. Only uncompromising, brave men who could push themselves into a deadly quagmire where winning was the only choice. Nevertheless, the Indian Army's core spirit was forged to protect the nation. Like 13 Punjab (JIND) and 54th Infantry Brigade's quagmire. Ladakh Scouts had its own share of struggle to bring HQ's attention to outposts like DBO. Capt. Rinchen and Col. Kapur kept persuading to bring DBO and Partapur Sector into the range of transportation to ease up the reinforcement at situational demand.

After briefing the force on battle positions Rinchen arrived at tactical headquarters. There he received a personal signal quoting "From the Big Tiger for the Nubra Tiger, I am proud of you and your brave Nonnos, you all have done a wonderful job. The frontiers of our mother country are safe in your strong hands. I am confident that under your able command you will give the 'Chinks' a befitting reply if they try to be funny this time. Your forced march from Baltistan to the Karakoram will go into the annals of Indian Military history. I wonder if your record of this great speed can ever be matched by any force in any Army of the world. Crossing Saser La at a height of approx 5,640 metres, at minus 40 degrees celsius, is one of the greatest feats of physical endurance and mental robustness. In my active soldiering of 24 years in various battles in North Africa, Razmak and Burma, I have not witnessed such grand soldiering as the one I saw in the last week of September. Well, done. I shall be seeing you and your boys soon."

Capt. Rinchen was a man of humble ethics, such a barrage of noble words for him was no less than a pot of treasure. This timely appreciation and gratitude between Rinchen and his Commander laid the foundation of a great friendship and deep respect they had for each other.

By the first week of October, the shadows of conflicts faded into an immediate ceasefire resulting in the uninvited war to end after hammering Pakistan enough to shame them in the battleground and on the international table. The potential risk on DBO Trijunction was averted and the situation was in full control. Colonel Kapur flew back to his headquarters in his chopper; he briefed Rinchen and gave him command of the post until the day he was needed again on the western front. Thus, Tiger was tasked to look after DBO Junction for now.

After a few days of returning to his HQ, Col. Kapur gave a thought of organising a little celebration for his men and called a thanksgiving meeting in his quarters and a get-together of all the officers, JCOs, and jawans present in that sector. A big bada khana was arranged. The Nubra Guards who had done commendable work were given appreciation from Ladakh Scouts and presented with prizes. A film show was arranged for the civil population and sweets were distributed. Such a benign gesture by the Commander made everyone happy. But somewhere the Commander himself was standing there with a half-pretended smile hanging inside some heavy thoughts he had there. Rinchen and his nonnos were present in that get-together; he saw that mild hidden sadness in the eyes of the Commander. Rinchen identified that anguish and it made him remember his own moment of despair which he had after the 1948 war ceasefire declaration.

Despite all this grand fanfare, Rinchen resonated that feeling of sorrow and discomfort on the face of the Commander. He decided to ask the Colonel the reason for his agony and braced his courage to walk towards him. In a jiffy, Rinchen realised to wait for a while and dropped his idea to ask why he looked so thoughtful and melancholy. Nevertheless, he resorted to silence and thought about asking him after the celebration.

Later, answer to his question came walking towards him, when Col. Kapur altered in a positive mood, he confided to him with his voluminous voice and said, "Rinchen, the Tiger of Nubra, mark my words; one day the efforts which you have made for the capture of Turtuk and Chorbat will come in handy.

Black Rock Fort will play a very important role in carrying out my plan of action, and your second MVC will be in your pocket. As and when I leave the command of the sector, I shall leave a full brief for the successor of my command."

Listening to Commander's words took Rinchen filled his mind many thoughts. He was compelled with the clear purpose of that sector which was standing mighty and high with waving the Tricolour.

Rinchen awakened his voice and said: "One day Turtuk and Chorbat will be under the flag of India, I believe in your idea, sir!"

The Commander smiled and replied, "Yes, Tiger, the day will be soon".

The suddenly erupted phrase of the Commander turned to be a sermon for Rinchen and the beginning of a prophetic legacy which was slowly being penned by fate inside the reality. Thus, the foundation of another valour was laid here.

❑

Chapter 9

An Unfathomable Soldier

The endeavour of the Himalayas took a whirl at an unwavering yet tentative course after 1967. Col. Kapur, the Commander of Partapur, was the precursor of the epitome whose name could be heard with the changes on the summit of the western frontier. Euphoric hospitality and nobility of Col. Kapur took a serene turn for Nubrans in the locality. The Commander of Partapur took initiative for the construction of the underground 12-bed hospital. A 45-metre long and 3.6-metre-wide underground area, which was approximately three metres deep, was dug out with the help of a bulldozer. The hospital was ready within a month. It later became a showpiece for the VIPs to visit. The jawans were delighted because in future there wouldn't be a day when had to look at the sky for medical help.

The GOC of the Division, Major Gen. K. George Bharat Singh, M C, who performed the opening ceremony of the hospital was most impressed not only with the building but with the comforts provided to the patients. Capt. Kalra, the young and dashing doctor in charge of the hospital, took great care in keeping the place running efficiently with the best tradition of the Army Medical Service. He was the most popular officer in the whole sector.

The quest for something productive for the surrounding led the Commander to continue his act of development covenant. The Tiger of Nubra, Rinchen, being the wingman for his work took the lead and carried various constructions including the building of a well-planned cinema hall and a canteen hall for get-togethers before and after the shows according to the will of the Commander. It became a popular spot for the troops and the local people who were thrilled to see the first film, 'Rajkumar'. The picture became so popular that it was shown a hundred times.

By the third quarter of the year, the Commander took up the mission to plant ten thousand saplings. Everyone in the area was made to adopt one sapling. Saplings turning into trees of testimony sang the blessing tale of (the then Commander) Colonel Kapur, who was worshipped as the King of Nubra. Colonel Kapur converted his Command and the Valleys of Nubra and Shyok into a real paradise.

One day, the Commander along with five officers and ten young hardy Ladakh Scouts Jawans climbed up the 'Charlie Fall' on the Ladakh range. By 6 pm, all of them climbed down close to the airfield. The next day, orders were issued for making a dam on the site. Within 15 days two-kilometre channel was made. Water became available to the troops near the bunker itself. The airfield too could be well watered thereafter that facilitated the landing of aircraft. Surplus water was given to the local people for irrigating their fields was additional benefit.

Colonel Kapur did not stop here. New tracks were made and new roads were constructed within the limited resources. There was never a dull moment in the sector. A gompa was made for the local Lama near the airfield which pleased the local people to the core. In Baigdangdo, he repaired the mosques for the Muslims and gifted food in the holy month of Ramzan. In April 1967, Rinchen moved with the Commander to the source of the river Nubra near Sasoma. It took them seven days to reach the Siachen Glacier defences. On his return from this recce, he ordered the defences of the area to be strengthened and Rinchen was given charge of the work. Shortly afterwards the Commander went away on a short leave and, on return, the first place he visited was the defensive line of the Siachen Glacier. He was over the moon and gave Rinchen a big pat on the back for the work so well done.

On 12 August, when the Commander proceeded towards the Headquarters; men and women of the Valley came out all the way to wish 'Juley' to the Commander. Such a warm welcome had never been given to any Commander in the past. But on reaching the Headquarters, one could see 'gloom' on the faces of the officers at the Headquarters.

The Brigade Major informed the Commander that his posting as the Chief of Staff Indo-China had come and that he had to report to Delhi forthwith which meant that the Nubrans would have no time to give a proper send off to the Commander who had brought changes to the land of courage. How could the people not be deprived of the right to give a warm send off to the man who had done so much for the Nubrans in just two and a half years? The news about his posting spread in the Nubra Valley like wildfire. Thousands of the Nubrans lined up in the 5-km route from the Headquarters to the Airfield to bid farewell to the dearest Commander whom they would never have a chance to meet again. At the airfield, the most touching scene was when the doctor arrived with all his patients to bid goodbye to the Commander who had given them not just a fine hospital but an opportunity to get treated well. 'Partapur would be like an empty anti-chamber without the King of Nubra,' Rinchen realised.

The brimming heat of change spawned from the snow land when in the first week of September 1967, a new Commander took over the command of the sector. From the day he joined, he had started behaving in a most ridiculous and spiteful manner as if he had been posted with a brief to find fault with everything that Colonel Kapur had done in the two and a half years of his command. He was covetous of the name 'Kapur' that wherever he saw the nameplate of the previous Commander, he ordered its removal with no time to spare. His doom came quickly when he converted the gompa that had been a gift of Colonel Kapur to his beloved Buddhist Nubrans, into a storehouse and a recreation hall. He never thought that this would become his last act of stupidity. The Jawans of the Ladakh Scouts and the Nubra Guards mutinied against him. When the higher authorities learnt about his wrong handling of the command affairs, he was promptly transferred and later sent on a premature retirement. The entire episode stank and sounds unsavoury and undignified. It was certainly not a moral anecdote but such incidents reminded the people that even a tiny act of good deed must be appreciated. Some stories should be narrated with a few pages of the pessimistic touch too to realise the worth of every sweat.

Since 1967, Major Chhewang Rinchen had become very popular in the Nubra Valley for his victories in both the wars and peace under the benign leadership of Colonel Kapur. But soon came a short period of grief when Colonel Kapur's successor acted indiscreetly to undo the environment forged by beloved Colonel Kapur. The people of Nubra Valley felt sore with what he did and raised their voice against him. How far Major Rinchen was involved in instigating the people of Nubra to protest was still an uncanny plot for many but within months the axe fell on him and nonetheless obedient officers like Rinchen knew where to stand for righteousness. In early February of 1968, during Rinchen's active duty, he got auspicious news of his fifth daughter's birth, whom he named Tsering Angmo. There are now five adorable children in his home who looked up to him.

At one instance due to sparkling and audacious activity by Rinchen which irked his senior, By the order of then General Officer Commanding, he was flown out of Baigdangdo in a helicopter to Lukung, a God-forsaken place near Pongong Tso (Lake) close to the Tibetan border as a 'punishment'. This added fuel to fire and even senior people like the Kalon of Leh, Rigzin Namgial Lonpo and the Head Lama of Sumur protested strongly and demanded the removal of the Sector Commander from Partapur forthwith. The locals' patience wilted; people raged up in flames of anger seeing their Tiger getting punished for being rightfully himself in his great service.

The General Officer Commanding who had sent Major Chhewang Rinchen into 'exile' had been posted out by then and his successor, realising the gravity of the situation, hastened to Partapur where he could meet important people and pacify them. Assuring that the Sector Commander, against whom they had raised their voice would be removed, the people became calm. The assurance given was carried out. After a few months, the honour of Major Rinchen was vindicated and he was posted back to Leh, and then transferred to 14 J&K Rifles at Tangdhar in the Srinagar Valley.

Major General Sukhwant Singh, who had been the Station Commander of Leh from 1967 to 1969, who had looked after the affairs of the Ladakh Scouts, was fond of Rinchen. Rinchen was in constant trouble because he found military discipline so irksome and had clashes with authority on many occasions. Major General Sukhwant Singh saw some soldierly potential in Rinchen's rebellious outlook. He justified his support to Rinchen every time in front of his superiors.

It was in April 1969 that Rinchen was posted from the Ladakh Scouts to 14 JAK RIF. He was posted at Chokibal in the Kashmir Valley field posting. On the dining-in-night in the Officers' Mess, Rinchen was offered whisky but he requested the Commanding Officer, Lt. Col. Ranjit Singh, to permit him to have his favourite drink, rum, which, he said, 'is a soldier's drink'. The Commanding Officer smiled and was good enough to agree to Rinchen's request as a special case, though normally rum was not served in the Officers' Messes. The party lasted till late hours. All the officers were in a jovial mood and talked about war and peace and all sorts of topics. Rinchen consumed nearly two dozen pegs all through he maintained sobriety and discipline.

At the end of the party, the Commanding Officer told Rinchen that next morning at 0500 hours they would proceed to Tangdhar. All the officers rushed to their rooms for a bit of sleep so did Rinchen. He had hardly slept for two hours when his orderly woke him up. Exactly at 0430hrs, he reported to the Commanding Officer with the Sten gun. Everyone was ready for the march.

Lt. Col. Ranjeet Singh was 48 years old but he was a tough and hard guy. The party marched through the snow, climbing a pass called Nasta Chun or Sadna Pass at a height of 3,000 metres. During March someone casually remarked, "This is the highest peak in the Kashmir Valley and many lives have been lost while crossing it." It appeared to be a challenge thrown to Rinchen. He could not swallow such a remark and retorted, "As far as I am concerned, climbing such a pass is no problem for me or any Ladakhi brother of mine, we live our normal life at such or even greater heights, stay up to 4,275 metres." The words of Rinchen flamed all soldiers which was a fascinating fact of every Ladakhi warrior. The treacherous atmosphere of high snowy ranges was paradise to such tough men forged under the Himalayan will.

After lunch, the entire party rolled down to the Tangdhar Valley and arrived at the Brigade Headquarters. The next day, as if to test his physical endurance and mental robustness, Rinchen was instructed to visit one of the highest posts in the region called Lippa Top at approx. 4,220 metres as his company was to be deployed there temporarily. Rinchen welcomed the order to climb up because nothing pleased him more than serving, under tough conditions. It was fun for him and a good experience for the future. He had always enjoyed undergoing specialised training at such heights. Moreover, he looked at it from an optimistic point of view. He felt that it would get him familiar with Kashmir's green valleys and mountains in contrast to Ladakh's barren, inhospitable, and rugged region.

Rinchen had spent nearly a year but used to visit his family at occasions, during his posting there, he was honoured with great news of birth of his sixth child and first son, all his daughters, then, got a little brother to cherish, born on 11 August, he was named Rinchen Wangchuk, even during his strict service, Maj. Rinchen always took time for his family. In October 1970, his battalion was transferred to Firozpur in West Punjab. During his stay with 14 JAK RIF till August 1971, he remained swamped undergoing training in 'warfare in plains or deserts and river crossing'. However, when summer approached, extreme heat became unbearable for him and he requested for posting back to the Ladakh Scouts that he was fortunate to get right in time. Rinchen found heat in the desert unbearable, it was not a fault in his basket to claim, child of the mountain could have hard times in scorch of desert sand eventually, and it was justice to his service to bring his potential in conditions where the snow tiger can fight with all his might.

On 13 August 1971, Rinchen joined his old Regiment, the Ladakh Scouts. The very same Regiment of snow warriors which was forged from his pioneering effort through the creation of his Nubra Guards. His next request was a posting in the Nubra Valley which was his home and where he had begun his Army career at the age of 17. In the Nubra Valley, he was familiar with every inch of land and he had climbed almost every notable peak and crossed every pass. Lt. Col. S.S.Tomar who was the Commandant of the Ladakh Scouts attached him to S.P. Company in the Nubra Sector.

The unjust wing again started to flow from the western side. This was just the time when clouds of war had begun to rumble on the horizon of every battle theatre. War with Pakistan became imminent. After a few weeks, when Major Prem Singh, the Second- in-Command, was posted out, Rinchen, being the senior-most was appointed Deputy Commander of the Ladakh Scouts in the Nubra Sector. The brick of foundation is now at the helm of Commanding his legacy again and that too at his home with full might.

The remnants of old metal were again fated to be forged for taking the shape of a spear from its former role of the sword. In the first week of September 1971, Major General S.P. Malhotra, General Officer Commanding, 3 Infantry Division, (later retired as Lt General and Army Commander, Northern Command) visited the Partapur Sector. He ordered Major Rinchen to reorganise the old Nubra Guards and give them special training in firing small arms. He had done so to prepare Rinchen and his Nubra Guards for the coming events. The guards who fearlessly acted as swords of frontiers against Pakistani troops had been now summoned again with more training and proper weapons. With great war experience, Rinchen carved out the spear from the sword he once used after creating it by his valley's soil and forging them in the flames of Indian Army training.

Meanwhile, in Partapur, the new Commander, Colonel (latest retired as Brigadier) Udai Singh, who took over the command of the Partapur sector in October 1971, restored all the name slabs and boards of Colonel Kapur in proper style within a week. This had a soothing effect on the agitated nerves of the Nubrans in due course and Rinchen's presence in Leh cooled down the rage of locals and Ladakh came back to normal.

Major Rinchen was able to enlist about 550 young volunteer Jawans whom he organised into four Companies called the Karakoram, Saser, Remo and Saltoro. Their training commenced on November 1 and terminated on 15 November, with a Passing out Parade during which the salute was taken by Major General S.P.Malhotra. The parade was organised with great pomp and show and all the trainees were smartly dressed in their local dress—goncha coat, skerak belt and pabu boots. The General

Officer Commanding was greatly impressed by their turn-out, high morale and firing skill. He asked Colonel Udai Singh, the Sector Commander and Major Rinchen, the Deputy Commander if they required any additional 'regular' battalion for the defence. Both of them assured the General that the Ladakh Scouts and the Nubra Guards would be able to undertake any operation in the sector and that no additional forces would be necessary. It was, of course, understood that one Infantry Battalion, along with a battery of artillery, which was earmarked to move into the sector for effective support during operations, would report soon for duty.

The General Officer Commanding was very pleased with Major Rinchen's organising capacity and qualities of leadership. Rinchen not only imparted basic military training and trained the Nubra Guards hard but also converted them into a well-knit, highly motivated, and cohesive professional group in the eyes of his superior Gen. S.P. Malhotra. In 1947, when a 17-year-old boy could train and led men with proper military elegance as a soldier, then it was not an impossible task for the same boy who turned 40 in his majestic uniform. It was not being said for no reason, 'beware of an old man in a profession where people usually die young.'

Towards the end of November 1971, Lt. Gen. Sartaj Singh, the Commanding Offficer of 15 Corps, visited the sector. Earlier, a message had arrived from the General Officer Commanding that the Corps Commander would like to hear, in brief, the history of the battles fought in the Valley, especially by the Nubra Guards.

Major Rinchen made a presentation with detailed charts in the crew room and briefed the Corps Commander for approximately half an hour. The General went away highly impressed by the confidence which the Ladakh Scouts and the Nubra Guards had in themselves. He instructed Major Chhewang Rinchen to organise an offensive operational exercise and thus get ready for any emergency.

Lt. General Sartaj Singh was known as a forceful and dynamic Commander in the Army hierarchy, with an intelligent grasp of the essentials. Once he was assured of the competence and capabilities of a senior officer working under him and was satisfied with the latter's plans of action, he would have no hesitation in delegating authority to fill in the details, keeping a watchful eye from above without undue interference.

Major General S.P. Malhotra, General Officer Commanding, 3 Infantry Division, was operationally responsible for the defence of Ladakh. He had to face two hostile neighbours, China and Pakistan. The area of responsibility, as far as Pakistan was concerned extended along the erstwhile ceasefire line from Baigdangdo in the Shyok river valley to the north of the Zojila. What China would do in case of a war between India and Pakistan was quite unpredictable. The General Officer Commanding, therefore, had to keep day and night vigil on the eastern borders as well to see that China did not come forward to assist Pakistan to fulfil obligations under the Sino-Pak treaty of 1963.

In short, General Malhotra had two-fold operational responsibilities against Pakistan or/and China, separately or simultaneously. He was, therefore, required to ensure the security of the Srinagar-Leh road which was the supply line for Leh and ultimately for the Partapur sector. He was also expected to be aware of the opportunities in taking counteroffensive action against Pakistan but simultaneously to ensure that the balanced defence posture was not disturbed at any time.

The region 18 was broken and rugged, cut by narrow gorges and ravines. The river valleys are narrow and the gradients steep. The temperature at the heights where operations were later conducted was as low as minus 40-degree celsius in winter. Indian military base of that region was bridged with Leh by a precipitous and indifferent pony track across Khardung La. An airfield had been constructed at Thoise in 1960 and this was the 'lifeline' for the maintenance of troops in the area. From Thoise, a jeep track ran along the Shyok River to within a few miles of Baigdangdo.

The area opposite Partapur Sector was held by Pakistan with three Companies of Karakoram Scouts with Wing Headquarters at Turtuk. Later, these were reinforced by two companies of mixed Karakoram and Gilgit Scouts. There were additional companies in the Kargil Sector. Pakistan had also mustered some reservists to make up the manpower at some posts. Pakistan had three 75mm guns, a section of 3.7" howitzers and six 3" mortars. Most of the weapons were deployed singly for snap shooting. The Pakistani posts, in varying strengths from a section upwards, were located at inhospitable heights. They were well entrenched and the likely approaches were blocked with mines.

Pakistan's forward posts close to the ceasefire line near Baigdangdo were connected with the military base at Gilgit and Skardu by a jeepable road up to Turtuk. From Turtuk, the supplies were sent to the posts by foot and animal transport. The terrain on the Pakistani side, as on the Indian side, was all rocky, mountainous, and steep. A small force could hold up a frontal offensive and no local outflanking movement was possible for either side unless troops crossed high mountain ranges and this could be done only on a limited scale.

The Nubra Valley was the gateway to the vast landmass of Ladakh. Its defence potentials had their own problems. As far as it was concerned, it was situated approx 140 km to the north of Leh, at a height of approx 3,000 metres. It was cut off from Leh which was situated in the Indus Valley by the Ladakh range. The Khardung La (5,602 metres) was the only pass and remained closed for six months during winter due to heavy snowfall.

The troops stationed in the sector were, therefore, maintained by the Indian Air Force either by landing or airdropping of all war materials including three-tonners and light vehicles. For movement within the sector, animal transport (yak, camel, mules, ponies, and donkeys) alone was utilised for carrying rations, beddings, ammunition, and other war equipment to the forward posts. The high posts were maintained by ponies or yaks. Helicopter service was used for carrying mail and evacuation of the sick.

On the Pakistan border, Indian posts, as well as those of Pakistan, were situated between the heights of 4,575 metres to 5,500 metres. One of the Pak posts, known as Gauri Shankar, was at a height of approx 5,610 metres.

There were occasions when, due to bad weather for many days and non-supply of the essentials by air, the troops had to depend on local vegetables, meat, and other supplies like sattu, pawai, thukpa and chang. The food articles were supposed to be more suitable during operational periods.

Arrangement for the supply of warm clothing had also improved considerably and was certainly much better than during the 1962 Chinese operations. Arms and ammunition issued to the troops within the sector were of the latest type and supplied in adequate quantity. Every company was authorised a Medical Officer of the rank of a Captain and a Nursing Assistant. The supply of medicines was adequate. Local hakims and vaidyas were also available.

The Regiment was also authorised by a special Signal Company Commander of the rank of Major. There were various types of signal equipment including long-range and modern sets. Most of the Jawans in the Signal Company were, however, from the plains. The locals were still under training.

When the Indo-Pak War broke out in 1971, it was started in East Pakistan. As the war heated up in East Pakistan, President Yahya Khan of Pakistan began to speak ill of India and shelling across the western borders started. He even threatened India with full-scale war and deployed his Army on the western front. One fine morning, he declared a state of emergency in Western Pakistan.

On December 3, 1971, India's Prime Minister declared, "India stands for peace but if war is thrust upon us, we are prepared to fight." On that very day, the Pakistan Air Force made pre-emptive airstrikes on the various airbases of India.

On the night of 3rd December, Major Rinchen was conducting night exercises with the Battalion of the Nubra Guards at Deskit. A telephone message was received from Colonel Udai Singh at 2330 hours, "War is declared. Warn the Ladakh Scouts and the Nubra Guards to be ready to move west on 4th morning." Rinchen closed the night training and issued warning orders to the Nubra Guards to be ready for the march.

Most of the Nubra Guards were keen to go to their homes to bring necessary warm clothing and rations. "If I permit them to go to their homes, they might not return within due time," thought Rinchen. He promised to issue them some rations and warm clothing on loan from the Ladakh Scouts stores. He completed the task during the night and by the morning of 4th December he was ready to move out with the troops.

On the morning of 4th December, various operational tasks were allotted to the Ladakh Scouts Battalion and the Nubra Guards, For deployment, four company were formed, the K Company was under the Command of Major Y.S. Thapa to move out of Partapur to forward posts to join D&G Companies. Further G Company was handed over to Major Ahluwalia. D Company came under the Command of Major S. K. Singh. Next in line was F Company, It was under the Command of Major G. Bisht. The company was established as a Reserve in the Nubra Valley in the Sasoma Area adjacent to the Chinese Posts. Capt. Shashi Anand of 1 Maratha LI (Jangi Paltan), was deployed in Ladakh Scouts as the Adjutant of the Partapur Sector, supposed to go with Maj. Bisht as his 2IC but few hours before the advance he was attached to the HQ for war duration. Finally, SP Company was under the Command of Capt. B.S. Juge. B. The structure of Ladakh Scouts was prepared here in consolidating manner.

Apart from Scouts, Nubra Guard was also in line for battle readiness. The first Coy was named after Karakoram ranges, likewise all Companies received their designation from summits standing around Nubra Valley. The Karakoram Coy Assault Group emerged under the Command of Shri C. Targis, (Retired as Naik). Later Saser Coy responsible for Line of Communication given to the Havaldar Tashi Mutup's (retired) command. Further, the Remo Coy was raised for Protection of the Airfield came to the Command of Naib Subedar Wangial (retired). And lastly Saltoro Coy in Reserve berthed under the Command of CHM S. Namgial (retired).

Cooperation of the people of the Nubra Valley was sought through the political leaders, Chhewang Rigzin, the Kalon of Leh, Kunzang Dorje, Major Rinchen's old father and Stanzin Tsering, the Headman, Shri Gurdev Singh, Assistant Commissioner of the Nubra Valley, located at Deskit, were ordered to supply necessary ponies and porters, and make other necessary arrangements. It was gratifying to note that the people, one and all, came forward at short notice to assist those who were in uniform, at the right time and the right place. The morale of each young man was high as he rushed to help the troops in whatever way he could, providing yaks, donkeys, or ponies for carrying, war equipment and rations to various points, putting aside all fears of enemy fire and shelling.

Major Rinchen most emphatically states how every family in Ladakh, whether Buddhist, Muslim, or Christian, provided at least one member for serving in the Army. If one brother was serving with the Ladakh Scouts, another joined the Nubra Guards and a third attended a pony on military duties or worked as a porter.

In Major Rinchen's family, one of his younger brothers, Phuntsog Namgial, was an MLC, another, Naik Sonam Dorje Singchan was serving, in the Ladakh Scouts as MT driver and the third, C. Norbu, was with the PWD. During the emergency, the last named joined the Nubra Guards. His servant also came forth with a pony for any duty. Rinchen's father, who was 82 years old, along with Phuntsog Namgial, younger brother of Chhewang Rinchen, went out to encourage the Nubrans to join the defence troops.

There were different types and trades of people in the Nubra Valley, like the Lamas, the Maulvis, and the Padris; businessmen; Government servants; farmers; and labourers. "When the freedom of the people is at stake, all of them work together and give full support to the Army.", Rinchen said. There were many gompas, some mosques and a few churches. Thousands of Lamas belonging to the yellow and the red sects, Maulavis and Mir Waizes, followers of Shia and Sunni sects and the few Christian families - all were engaged in prayers - in gompas, mosques and churches - for the victory of the Indian Army in the coming confrontation.

The force known as the 'DHAL' force which was placed under the command of Major Rinchen for operations, comprised four Ladakh Scouts Rifle Companies, D, G, K, and SP and four Companies of the Nubra Guards, as mentioned earlier.

Rinchen set off with the main force on December 5 with the war cry, 'Ki Ki So So Lhargyalo' (Victory to the God), and reached Baigdangdo by midnight after covering a long and tedious journey of 40 km by vehicles from Partapur to jeep-head Nullah Pachetang and another 40 km on foot.

Rinchen called all the Company Commanders at No. 7 post at Baigdangdo for the final briefing and orders at the Assembly Area – Nagpo Thang - on the Baigdangdo Nullah. Colonel Udai Singh, the Sector Commander, was also there to finalise points of strategy. The briefing started at 1900 hours. There were five Company Commanders and two Medical Officers.

The first important decision to be taken was regarding the approach to the Pak Chalunkha defence complex. There were two approaches available - one from the right across the mountainous countryside and the other along the valley riverbed. To mount strong force on the western frontier, Rinchen remembered the wise words of his former senior Col. Kapur. While recalling his words, everything was making sense to him. The preparation Colonal made during his stay for laying siege on Chalunkha and Turtuk front had turning to be a hidden boon for him but it was a long way to go before he arrived on rocks that battlefront. Rinchen now was enlightened deeply about his next move; he was just waiting to grab a proper chance before moving with his eruption of will.

All Company Commanders, except Shri C. Targais of the Nubra Guards, were in favour of attacking the Pak positions from the riverbed side. Major S.K. Singh, Major Ahluwalia, Major Thapa, and Capt. Juge, all wanted to take the riverbed route and avoid the tough climbing of the steep slopes of the mountains. But Rinchen was strongly opposed to the idea. He pointed out the risks involved. The enemy must have already covered the riverbed approach and gaps by laying mines, setting up barbed wire fencing and mounting roadblocks.

Moreover, there would always be a danger of facing firing by the enemy forces from the ridges on either side of the riverbed. He selected the approach of Pt 'V' to capture Pt 18,402, the highest Pak-occupied post on the front and then roll down to the Chalunkha complex. Rinchen had already tried this approach twice—once during August 1965 on instructions from Colonel Kapur and again in September 1971 during patrolling. Colonel Udai Singh agreed with Rinchen's arguments and approved his plan for an indirect approach. Rinchen sighted his chance with the approved action of strategy. All Company Commanders became convinced that Major Rinchen's technique of indirect approach was most suitable for the Partapur Front terrain.

By the beginning of December 1971, when Major Rinchen was given the command of the Task Force to launch an assault on Baltistan during the Indo-Pak War which took place in that month, he had the experience of guerrilla warfare in the mountains extending over 23 years. He had also crossed the 40th year of his life and had acquired maturity of judgement and clarity of tactical concepts. For some past, he had been nursing certain ideas to augment the fighting efficiency of the Jawans under his command.

The ideas were not only unorthodox and unconventional but positively revolutionary in concept and implementation and would have been normally unacceptable in the Army way of thinking which often would go by rules and regulations blindly. Major Rinchen was lucky in one way; not only his immediate boss but even those who were higher up in the long chain of command had full confidence in his qualities of leadership. His deep understanding of the tactical and strategic problems involved in mountain warfare were noticed and believed. That is why when he proposed to introduce certain radical changes in the outfit of his jawans just before launching the attack against the enemy to make them more nimble and agile, they accepted his ideas readily and agreed to give them an honest trial.

Rinchen discarded the steel helmet for the Balaclava cap and ammunition boots for pabo shoes; the water bottle no longer contained aqua pura but a new drink, and a load of ammunition and baggage was halved. He made his jawans 'light-capped, light-footed, light-armed and light-bagged'. His way of engaging the enemy depended on superior mobility and course of agility in harsh snow-laden areas. And he was right in his way since his perception was long-sighted for aiming to defeat the enemy without making his own stand a liability with unnecessary load for his nonnos. He greatly shaped the high-altitude warfare ability of the Indian Army which he gets little credit for.

The greatest show of war in mountains was laid with the will to fight against odds since a soldier fighting the enemy in such a region has always needed to confront the weather as the primary enemy and later the mortal bodies with whom he is fighting. Amusingly for Rinchen and his nonnos, the atmosphere of Ladakh and Himalayas were boon, their immunity in such a treacherous region made them apex predators in snow and Rinchen did not doubt that.

Regarding the various changes which Rinchen introduced, the then GOC, Maj. Gen. S.P. Malhotra noticed that these tactics worked universally at his command and not restricted only to Nubra Guards. Rinchen's tactics prevailed so efficiently that it was, therefore, difficult to say as to which commander or any other officer in uniform suggested which changes and at what level of command were these approved and when. Suffice to say that such changes and innovations worked to the advantage of troops in the high altitude and mountainous areas by time of reinforcements as the war was at its peak and every man in Northern command pushing his limit to serve the force.

These dynamic yet unorthodox ways of Major Chhewang Rinchen, few who understood their effectiveness observed that, Major Rinchen had a feeling that wearing a steel helmet was not only unnecessary but positively harmful for fighting in the mountains for various reasons. Because of its heavyweight, it slowed the speed of a jawan while ascending or descending the steep slopes of mountains. As it was metallic, chances for frostbite to the head, especially nose and ears, became greater.

More important, while climbing up or rolling down, the accidental fall of a single steel helmet, rolling down the slope to the bottom hill, could make such a terrific noise, echoing and re-echoing and renting, the air in the dead silence of the night that even a dozing and snoring, sentry at the enemy post would 'stand-to-attention' and shout, "Dushman! Dushman!" The assaulting party would lose the advantage of surprise. The steel helmet was, therefore, replaced by the Balaclava cap which was lighter and warmer.

Later, regarding footwear, Major Rinchen ordered the jawans to deposit the ammunition or jungle boots and exchange them for the Ladakhi pabos which were light but pretty-warm and would protect the feet from frostbite. He asked the Headman of the village to help them in getting pabos in exchange for ammunition boots from the villagers who were exceedingly happy to give away their pabos and get ammunition boots in return. Some officers who did not take his advice seriously suffered from frostbite during the campaign.

Further Major Rinchen's experience was that water in the water bottle always froze after climbing a few hundred metres, especially on cold nights when the temperature went down to minus 20 to 40 degree Celsius. He asked the Quarter Masters of the various Companies to issue some extra rum, get it mixed with water and fill all 'water bottles' with this new drink. It did not freeze and proved to be the elixir of life for the jawans who otherwise shivered with cold during night marches. It also warmed up everyone while launching the assault.

It may be recalled that on the Kargil front, where there was an acute shortage of water, water in Jerry cans brought by the jawans from the nullahs far down below to the battle sites at heights often got frozen. At times, the Jerry cans would burst forth and the jawans had to carry uncovered blocks of ice with their hands.

The bedding was an essential issue and every jawan carried one sleeping bag and two blankets with some additional bedding of considerable weight. Major Rinchen instructed his jawans to carry one sleeping bag and one blanket between two of them and in no case carry any extra bedding for the simple reason that they were not going to sleep during nights and did not require much bedding for rest during day time. Moreover, he expected them to get the gift of bedding from the enemy jawans when the latter was put out from the bunkers.

Major Rinchen also halved the quantity of ammunition that every jawan was required to carry with him as per the authorised scale. This reduced the load considerably. He told his brave jawans to depend more on hand grenades and bayonets and indirect approach to the enemy posts by going from behind the enemy post and entering it by using the secret approach route.

He told them to use ammunition only as the last resort.

His instructions were 'minimum expenditure of ammunition - one round one man and no more - and maximum use of hand grenades and bayonets.' Moreover, he wanted that his men used against the Pakistani forces the ammunition they had earlier captured in the offensive from the posts vacated by the Pakistani troops

Lastly, Major Rinchen exhorted his jawans to launch the assault by shouting the war cry, 'Ki Ki So So Lhargyalo.' "You are the tigers of Ladakh and Nubra; I will give you the roar, that shall galvanise you into reckless dare-devils. Victory shall be yours," said he. His pitch of voice to his fellow soldiers was not ordinary speech. In tactical scenarios the war planning was done and it was the beginning of first phase against the Assault of Turtuk. According to the plan, the first task was to capture Picquet V summit and Pt 18,402 (5,609 metres), the next task was to lead Advance to capture Chalunkha Defence Complex, the most important part of the strategy. Preparation was completed and from higher ranks Order of March were dispatched to the troops. Tracing through the orders. The troops were tasked to move at 1500 hours with the planned structure comprised of G Company, Rinchen's Order 'O' - G Group, S P Company Element, K. Company, and Medical Element. Companies of the Nubra Guards less 1 Platoon, 75 Porters from Baigdangdo and 1 Platoon of the Nubra Guards.

Now the chronicle begins with Rinchen's First Objective -to achieve Pt 18,402, the task of capturing Pt 18,402, the highest post ever to be captured in the world, was assigned to Major S.S.

Ahluwalia whose company was leading. One of his platoons was commanded by Naib Subedar P. Angdu who was given the task of supporting the attack on Pt 18,402 from the right ridge, while Major Ahluwalia was to launch the offensive with 2 platoons.

The 400-men column, marching in single file, was very long indeed and it was difficult to keep control and regulate the movement, especially while climbing the steep hills at night. Rinchen could keep watch till the last light but, thereafter, due to sheer steep height, altitude sickness, difficulty in breathing, headache and cold, some people began to drop out, mostly the non-locals. The signal equipment and wireless set which were handled by the non-locals had to be shifted to the locals.

The Dhal Force was scheduled to capture Pt 18,402 by midnight but as climbing was tough, the time calculation went wrong. The attacking party could reach by midnight only close to Picquet 'V' which was just below Pt 18,402. A very light red firing went up from the Pak post at Pt 18,402. Rinchen contacted Major Thapa and asked him to cover Picquet "V'. Troops were rushed to occupy it before it got alert.

The Pak troops which had learnt of the pending attack by the Indian troops started firing guns from Pt 18,402, followed by 2" mortars. After some time 3"/ 81 mm mortars were also fired from the direction of Chalunkha.

About 75 percent of Rinchen's troops were 'green'. They were taking part in an operation for the first time. Only 25 percent were his old seasoned Ladakh Scouts and Nubra Guards who had the experience of fighting in 1948, 1962 and 1965. In the first hour of heavy shelling by the enemy, troops who were taking part for the first time became panicky and tried to take cover for shelter. It all devolved upon the Commanders to take initiative and boost up the morale of the troops by giving pep talks and raising slogans or by giving firm orders promptly and by ordering fire at the correct time.

Rinchen ordered Havaldar Nurbu of the MMG section to engage the LMG firing from Pt 'V' to facilitate the advance of Major Ahluwalia towards the objective. As heavy firing was coming from Pt 18,402, Major Ahluwalia was instructed not to approach the objective from the front. He was told to move with one platoon silently from the left, go behind Pt 18,402 and wrest possession of the Pakistan line of communication to the top, while the rest of the troops were to continue keeping the enemy engaged by firing from their present position.

The next morning, by five o'clock, K Company had secured Pt 'V'' completely. At that critical moment, Rinchen ordered the platoon of the Nubra Guards which was at the tail end of the long column of porters to shout at the top of their voice for the Pakistanis at Pt 18,402: "Hands up and surrender otherwise you will be killed." The loud shouting by the Nubrans echoed and re-echoed in heavy snow-covered rocky hills. The attention of the Pak troops at Pt 18,402 was diverted and Major Ahluwalia got the opportunity to get behind, enter the Pak post on the quiet, cut off their line of communication, enter their bunkers and trenches and throw hand grenades and make a bayonet charge. Many Pak soldiers were killed in the bunkers and trenches and the remaining, along, with the JCO, fled away towards the Administrative Post.

Rinchen, all the while, was awaiting news of the success from Major Ahluwalia. It took over an hour, waiting in extremely cold weather with snow all around. Hands, ears, and feet were getting cold. Major Thapa waiting next to Major Rinchen was shivering badly with cold. Rinchen opened his water bottle and gave him a peg to drink, asking, "Guess, what is in the drink?" "Arak, I believe?" replied Thapa. Rinchen gave him another peg.

Thapa felt warm and said, "Oh, it is brandy, mixed with water." Rinchen then asked Thapa, "What is the drink in your bottle?" "It is rum mixed with water", replied Thapa. "Then, carry on, whenever you feel thirsty or cold, that is your drink on these heights.", was the advice given by Rinchen to Thapa.

Major Thapa was wearing pabo shoes and that is why he did not suffer from frostbite, thus saving his feet. Capt. Juge who was the Mortar Officer suffered from severe cold and frostbite for he was wearing jungle boots. As much it seemed unorthodox and local but Rinchen's way was by his ability to function in such a hellish environment.

In the morning hours, Rinchen could hear hand grenades bursting at Pt 18,402. Rinchen knew that the post had been stormed by Major Ahluwalia. It was apparent that the indirect approach had served the purpose. He ordered MMGs and 2" mortars to stop firing on Pt 18,402 lest his own man was killed. He took over the MMG from Havaldar Norbu and started firing on the enemy troops fleeing from Pt 18,402 and running towards the Administrative Post. The Pak troops from the Administrative Post opened fire in retaliation and heavy firing continued for about 15 minutes.

Then, there was the war cry, 'Ki Ki So So Lhargyalo'. This was the success signal and Rinchen rushed to Pt 18,402 with the rest of the troops. It was 0700 hours and Major Ahluwalia had occupied the post with the help of 18 dare-devil NCOs and jawans. Five Pak soldiers were killed and one man with an LMG was taken as a prisoner. There were no casualties on the Indian side except that three nonnos suffered minor injuries. Rinchen sent a runner to call Capt Sujan Singh, the Medical Officer, and his medical attendant but it was learnt that the doctor and his medical attendant had returned to Baigdangdo at 0400 hours as they were down with severe cold and sickness Under the circumstances, the injured soldiers were given some local treatment and then sent to No.7 post at Baigdangdo on the manpack.

L/Naik Ghulam Hasan of the Pakistan Army who had been made a prisoner of war at Pt 18,402 was interrogated. He gave some valuable information regarding the strength, disposition, arms and ammunition, and approaches to their post. As per his statement: There was one wing of Karakoram Scouts consisting, of 3 Companies, each consisting of 4 Platoons. There were approximately 2 Companies of Razakars, one Platoon of 3"/81 mm mortar and one Platoon of MMGs and The Wing Commander was a Major and the troops were mostly from Gilgit and Hunza, while a few were local. The Razakars were all local and were issued with .303 rifles.

Initially, his statement was not believed but later, it was found that he was correct in whatever he had said.

On the morning of December 8, at 0700 hours, when Rinchen was on the top of Pt 18,402, he observed the Pak-occupied area right from CP, OP Ridge to Turtuk and Chalunkha. The Pakistani posts and lines of communication were clearly visible. Next, he looked back towards the Nubra Valley. The Indian Army Headquarters at Partapur and the Airfield at Thoise were clearly palpable. Obviously, the Pakistani troops had chosen to occupy that point because of its importance from the tactical point of view.

As Rinchen looked down from Pt 18,402 to the Pak Administration Post which was hardly 650 metres away, he could see several trenches and bunkers. In the centre, it was obviously the cookhouse as smoke was coming out of its chimney. By then, the enemy at the Administration Post had learnt that their post at Pt 18,402 had been captured by the Indian troops and they lost their morale. About 50 Pakistani soldiers seemed to be rushing to 'stand-to-position'. Rinchen asked Capt Juge to contact the mortar section at point No. 6 and order them to engage the enemy at the Administrative Post with shelling. The MMG was also fired. The shots neutralised the enemy troops which got panicky and began to run helter-skelter, leaving their trenches and bunkers.

At about 0900 hours, Rinchen gave the success signal to the Commander of the Sector, Colonel Udai Singh, who congratulated the troops on their success. The congratulatory message given by the Sector Commander went a long way in boosting the morale of the forces under the command of Rinchen.

The troops rested the whole day on the reverse slopes of Pt 'V' and Pt 18,402. In the evening they arrived at Pt 18,402 and started rolling down at about 1830 hours. The order of March was released comprising of K Company under Major Y.S. Thapa followed by O Group of Rinchen joining with Nubra Guards, G Company, and porters.

The descent was as steep and tough as the climbing on the other side approach to Pt 18,402 ft. It took two and a half hours to climb down by approx 300 metres. At 2200 hours they surrounded the Administrative Post but there was no sign of the enemy. The Jawans of Rinchen entered the bunkers with bayonets and hand grenades and made a thorough search from bunker to bunker. As the troops from the Administrative Post had withdrawn, Major Thapa who commanded 'K' Company faced no resistance when he launched the attack. A lot of war equipment and other stores were found at this post, 50 sets of ECC clothing, bedding, all made in the USA and China, Hundreds of blankets and sleeping bags, bukharies fitted in the bunkers. Many utensils, including, pressure cookers, cooked dal and puris for breakfast and huge quantity of ammunitions.

After detailing troops for patrolling duty in the surrounding area, Rinchen said to his officers and men, "You can use Pak bunkers, bukharies, beddings and enjoy good food, as the Pakistani soldiers have left everything in a hurry and had no time to poison the food." The meat was cooked and a lot of rum was consumed. Even the porters enjoyed good food and were given blankets. One of the bunkers, perhaps used by the officers, had American sleeping bags and air mattresses.

All the troops were given complete rest for the night till stand-to report next morning.

December 9-10 were the victory days. Early morning, on 9th December, when the troops assembled, Rinchen enquired from all the Commanders including, the Commander of the porters if they were fit to advance. It was reported that a few jawans of Ladakh Scouts and Nubra Guards and a few porters were suffering from minor frostbite on hands and feet. Rinchen checked the cases personally. Those suffering were detained with the Administration Column along with the porters.

Major Ahluwalia was also detained. Capt. Juge, despite being frostbitten, insisted on joining the forces for the advance against the final objective.

At 0930 hours, Rinchen proceeded along the ridges, with his 'O' Group (Order Group) towards the Chalunkha defence complex, crawling, and hiding so as not to be seen by the enemy, till they reached a point from where he could see the entire Chalunkha defence line. Through binoculars, he observed the area and the activities there for about half an hour. The approach to the post was only at one point and that was from the Chalunkha Nullah site. There was no other approach. That posed a big problem that Rinchen had been always keen on reaching a higher level and then rolling down close to the enemy's stronghold but in this case, there seemed to be no other alternative except the Nullah approach, which, Rinchen felt, would be risky as the enemy was most likely to have laid mines or set up roadblocks.

Rinchen decided to lead the assault himself along with Major Thapa. Two platoons were picked up from K and G Companies and the Nubra Guards. One Platoon from each Company was kept in reserve. After lunch, he briefed all the troops for the coming night attack. The Jawans looked fresh after a full night rest and their morale was unimaginably high.

Rinchen ordered Capt. Juge to instruct the mortar section at No. 6 Post to fire mortars on the enemy defences. The mortars fell very close to the enemy's position but in retaliation, not a single shot was fired from the Pak side, nor was there any sign of movement in that area. "It could be either of two possible alternatives," Rinchen pondered. He mumbled, "Either the enemy troops have escaped or they have received good training and are well-disciplined. They have not panicked and, sure enough, are not going to come out of their trenches and bunkers till the right moment." Rinchen instructed the mortar section to stop shelling and took the bold decision to launch an assault, not frontal but through an indirect approach.

There was a water channel through which water was carried to the Chalunkha defences and the channel was running through the centre of the Pak stronghold. It was found to be dry as the villagers had stopped the water supply just before the winter had set in. The observation of the circumstances and utilising every source made Rinchen a soldier who never missed a chance and risk his men's life. Rinchen instructed Major Thapa to move along the water channel and enter the main Pak position from behind unless there was some obstacle along the channel. Naib Subedar C. Angdus and Naib Subedar A. Rahman were to assist him.

The grim nature of the Turtuk complex was gradually turning into the covenant of sharp ignition of the enemy movement but Rinchen was in no mood to let the enemy misadventure similarly how they did in 1948 on the Karakoram frontier. Fortifying his claws and veins, Rinchen was about to deliver everything he had. The Tiger was about to roar and charge that he didn't want to carry a regret to home.

❑

Chapter 10

Turtuk Under Tiger's Shelter

The wind was uncanny, composed and extremely like a mystery to predict. The atmosphere was fighting and agitating with the warm breath of soldiers standing with fire in the eyes. The muscles turned mighty metal, flesh forged in ferocious flame, and blood was blazing bravery in all men on vanguard behind Chhewang Rinchen with the fistful of Ladakh Scouts and Nubra Guards. The zealous fortitude of Rinchen and his men continued in the direction of the battle. Hostility on the ground towards the drumming enemy lines was fanning the ember to get flamed, despite everything Rinchen continued to prey on enemies. Rinchen was in communication with both Major Thapa on one side and Colonel Udai Singh on the other hand. Major Thapa informed Rinchen over the wireless that his group had entered the perimeter of the Pak defences, but, while he could see trenches and bunkers there was no sign of enemy troops. Colonel Udai Singh flashed good news to Rinchen, "Congratulations, Rinchen. All India Radio announced that the Ladakh Scouts in Partapur Sector had captured the highest post, Pt. 18,402, the highest ever captured in the world history of warfare and were advancing like storm and thunder."

But soon, misfortune knocked at the door, contact with Major Thapa was cut off. The situation had become worse when the enemy stationed at Chalunkha opened fire with mortars and machine guns. Rinchen's troops faced heavy firing, from all sides - from the left and the left top, from the right spur and the right from across the river. It became most distressful.

It was most encouraging when Thapa's voice was heard again, informing Rinchen that his team had entered the enemy bunkers and a few enemy Jawans had been killed and a JCO was captured. Rinchen was getting impatient to join Major Thapa but he could not stir out and advance because of heavy MMGs firing from all around. The signalman was hit by a burst of MMG fire. Luckily, he received only minor injuries on his leg. The wireless set had to be removed from his shoulders and put on the back of Rinchen's orderly. Rinchen tried to do his best to give field dressing to the signalman but he found it difficult to do so during heavy shelling from all the sides. There was no second to spare as time was having the entry card to hell.

"Oh, how I wish two bold and fearless Jawans could crawl to the enemy post with hand grenades and silence the gun post!" mused Rinchen. Sepoy Dorje and Ali readily offered their services and went crawling close to the enemy MMG post. They threw hand grenades but the MMG gun post was strongly defended and the grenades went ineffective. Next, Naik Fateh Mohammad offered his services to do the job. He said, "Kafironko to main khatam kar dunga; mujhe hathgole chahiye." Rinchen gave him one box of hand grenades that had been captured from the Pak forces at Pt 18,402.

Initially, Naik Fateh Mohammad also failed to destroy the bunkers in which the MMG was stationed. He requested more grenades and they were dispatched to him swiftly.

At last, success was achieved and the gun was silenced when the midnight about 0200 hours. Green 'V' light signal came from the top gun post with a war cry. No sooner had the guns been silenced than Rinchen with his party rushed forth to join Major Thapa. The reserve column which had been held up in the Nullah also advanced.

The main post had been captured but troubles were not yet over. Though a few guns had been silenced, quite a few others installed by the enemy in the surrounding areas, especially those from across the river Shyok, continued to fire. Colonel Udai Singh became apprehensive of a counter-attack. Major Rinchen, however, played cool and did not get panicky. "Rest assured, Sir, the situation is well under control. You will soon hear some good news," said Rinchen to the Sector Commander on the wireless. Just then, two jawans arrived with a message from Naib Subedar Angdus, informing Rinchen that 'three crew members of the enemy MMG had been killed and the MMG captured.' It was rather unbelievable because not a single shot had been fired nor had any hand grenade burst. Later, Rinchen learnt that Naib Subedar S.Wangdu, Havaldar Stobdan, Havaldar Norbu, and Sepoy Sundus had done advanced crawling, taking advantage of the enemy firing.

Whenever the guns were fired, they advanced and whenever the guns stopped, they took position quietly. Thus, they managed to reach the enemy bunkers and kill all the crew members with bayonets; Havaldar Stobdan was in such a frenzy that he immediately seized the MMG and threw it in the Chalunkha Nullah. When, later, he was asked,

"Why did you do so?". His answer was, "The gun was totally damaged. It was of no use to us."

Soon, Major Rinchen was in the Pak Command post with Major Thapa. He asked the Guard Commander to produce the senior-most prisoner of war but no amount of interrogation could get any useful information from him. He was placed under arrest and kept in a separate bunker under a sentry.

At about 0600 hours, a runner came from Naik Fateh Mohammad with news that the Pak soldiers had made a hole in the top of their bunker and were showing their hands. When Rinchen reached close to the bunker, he noted that the Pak troops had stopped firing and were shouting, "We want to surrender." Rinchen ordered his men to stop firing and throwing hand grenades on the enemy bunkers and shouted, "If you want to surrender, throw your weapons." They started throwing their arms out of the holes in the roof of their bunkers. These included two machine guns, one 2" mortar, a few rifles and Sten guns and two V light pistols.

Rinchen again shouted, "Throw all grenades and bayonets and come out one by one holding your hands up." As they came out in a file, Rinchen asked one of the jawans from Naik Fateh Mohammad's Platoon to search everyone. One jawan of the Ladakh Scouts who had got furious because the whole night he had suffered from severe cold and whose feet had been frostbitten shot down a Pak prisoner of war and was going to shoot another when Rinchen shouted and ran towards him. He snatched away the rifle from his hand and gave him a hard slap. Addressing, his jawans, he said, "Remember, once the Pak soldiers have surrendered, they are our guests and friends." Despite being a ruthless fighter on the war front, Rinchen had the strength to transition his anger into compassion. His flexibility under the natural virtue of righteousness earned him respect from all directions.

Rinchen has certain high ideals regarding the treatment to be meted out to the prisoners of war, the then Army Chief Sam Manekshaw had such disposition of fighting warlike brutal predator but also protecting and providing hospitality whoever sought shelter under his wings, this lone edict of the Indian Army soldier made them higher than any warriors, Rinchen approached the Pakistani prisoners and apologised to them for the unfortunate incident. He shook hands with them one by one and congratulated them for their good fighting spirit. "You are all brave and I appreciate your unbounded courage and absolute loyalty to your country. It was your duty to fight for your country as best as you could and you did so. Now, since you have surrendered, you are our guests and friends," said Rinchen, addressing the prisoners of war. Later, he asked Targis, the Commander of a Nubra Guards Company, to detail an escort guard for the prisoners and gave him instructions to look after them with all courtesy.

There had been severe fighting for over ten hours to capture Pt 18,402 and Chalunkha defence complex but the Indian troops had surprisingly suffered no casualties. This was something highly creditable and Rinchen ascribes it to his adoption of the indirect approach technique and the guerrilla tactics of Chhatrapati Shivaji Maharaj.

Immediately after, Rinchen instructed Naib Subedar C. Angdus to go with his platoon to capture the Administrative Post and Chalunkha village which was close by. Surprisingly, not a single civilian could be seen in the village, for everyone had run away fearing that the Indian troops would ill-treat them. This impression had been created in their mind by the retreating Pak soldiers.

Naib Subedar Angdus had no alternative left but to surround the village and make a search from house to house. Only one JCO who was wounded and had been left behind by the fleeing Pakistani soldiers was found hiding in one of the houses.

Time was running and each second was crucial, by 1100 hours, the entire Chalunkha defence complex was under the occupation of the Indian troops. Rinchen's troop got a sizeable cache of enemy equipment in their hands, like Rifles of 303 calibre with 75 ammunition which were to be distributed among the Razakars, cash - about Rs. 8,000, some important service documents, transistor sets, plenty of ammunition, ration, and clothing, and plenty of signal equipments.

All these days, Rinchen had not received any news regarding Capt. Kalia who had been detailed to proceed to Tebedo Nullah on December 8 along, with a platoon. They had crossed the river Shyok the same night with the help of porters belonging to Baigdangdo, especially one Sikandar who was an expert in making local boats with Jerry cans. It was Sikandar who was primarily responsible for the successful crossing of all troops across the river during that cold and dark night. Capt. Kalia had failed to keep contact with Rinchen as his signal equipment had fallen and got damaged. He was supposed to assault the Pak CP and OP on December 9 and 10 simultaneously with the battle for the Chalunkha defence complex.

It was only when Rinchen was looking all around through binoculars that he observed a group of soldiers rolling down from the ridge Tebedo to Pakistan OP. How happy he was to note that it was the platoon of Capt. Kalia! Rinchen could see that about twenty Pak soldiers came forward with white flags and lined up before Capt. N.K. Kalia as soon as he arrived at the OP. The entire personnel of the enemy mortar platoon surrendered to Capt. Kalia along with huge quantities of arms, ammunition, and clothing. The Pak CP post had already been vacated during the night of December 9 and 10. There had been no fighting at OP and CP; it was just a silent battle that resulted in the success of the Indian forces. Rinchen immediately rushed with a section of troops to reinforce Capt. Kalia.

The bugle of victory had begun to resound. The first phase of capturing the Chalunkha complex was thus completed with a categorical success. During this phase of assault, a great deal of capturing enemy assets was witnessed, followingly 40 prisoners of war surrendered including 2 JCOs, 38 ORs with four Razakar civilians, apart from prisoners, six mortars of two and three inches, six machine guns, 63 rifles, pile of ammunition, six months' worth of ration for Dhal Force and large number of other war equipment came under Rinchen's possession.

Arms and ammunition surrendered by the Pakistani troops proved to be very useful to the Indian troops. By just turning their nozzles and barrels from east to west the rifles could be used against the Pakistani forces, in case the latter planned a counter-attack.

December 11 was an Administration Day for the entire Dhal Force. The entire day was devoted to the re-organisation of the troops and the evacuation of casualties including frostbite cases to Sector Headquarters. Major Ahluwalia, Capt. Juge, and Capt.

Kalia were also evacuated to the General Hospital.

Major Rinchen expressed his special gratitude to the helicopter pilots who flew over 6,100 metres high Khardung La from dawn to dusk. Unmindful of bad weather and enemy air and ground attacks, they cleared all the wounded and frostbite cases within 48 hours, making 70 sorties from Leh to forward posts on improvised landing grounds. Especially the services rendered by Flight Lts. M.P. Singh, Lahu, and Dhillon. Flight Lt. Behl was attached to the Dhal Force as ATC but his services had never been sought by Rinchen for any air support except on the last day of war, i.e., December 17, when Rinchen had planned to mount an attack on Piun, the Pak Sector Headquarters.

Rinchen has a fondness for the Brigade Major Chandramani of the Grenadiers, who was a dynamic officer with a cool temperament. During the entire operation, he turned out to be a key man between the Dhal Force and the Brigade Headquarters. Most regularly, he sent information about the welfare of the Ladakh Scouts and the Nubra Guards to their families in distant villages. In particular, he sent special runners to inform the old parents of Rinchen how well their son was faring on the front. Basically, he handled the network of HUMINT providing the needed communications between troops.

The entire war scenario was mounting in scale day by day, an inch of dominance against the enemy had strategic impact, the war has entered in its second phase. December 12 was the day of re-organisation of troops, coordination of supporting arms and briefing of the troops which were detailed for the next offensive. The task was designed and plan was ready to be carried out. The initial plan was to lead offensive charge against Turtuk on the left bank of the river Shyok and another offensive against Thang on the right bank of the river Shyok simultaneously. The tactical manoeuvring here was to corner the enemy post from both choke points.

Further, the troop got their comprehensive Order of March, according to the drawn task, D and G Companies and one Platoon of Nubra Guards was ordered to advance along the left road to Turtuk. Meanwhile K Company with 2 Platoons tasked to advance along with Nubra Guards right road to Thang, addition to its Mortar Platoon mobilised to charge along the main road as a supporting arm for both offensives during the hour of assault.

The patrolling teams which Rinchen had sent, on the night of December 12, towards Turtuk and Thang had brought some important information regarding enemy dispositions. The Pakistani troops had established roadblocks and were digging defences at Ramdo Nullah at Turtuk on the left flank. The locals had set up roadblocks opposite Turtuk village top and river bed.

On 12th December, the Indian troops resumed their advance and established their defence close to Ramdo Nullah from where they could study the Pakistani defence preparations more closely. It was clear that the Pakistani troops were being reinforced for making a counter-attack. Rinchen passed on a message to the Sector Commander that he would like to spend the night studying the enemy dispositions in a greater detail and might have to postpone the attack towards the dawn.

The supporting arm moved close to the enemy defences till

Pak Wing Headquarters at Turtuk were within the range of the Indian mortar section. The priority was given to destroying the roadblocks to Turtuk with mortars so that the troops could advance and launch an attack on Turtuk on December 13/14 night without hindrance. The shelling started at 1600 hours to destroy the roadblocks near the Turtuk axis and harass the Turtuk top.

In further orders, Naib Subedar Angdus was detailed to clear the Turtuk top. While Major Thapa was asked to clear the road axis towards Thang, at last, Major Rinchen, along with Major S.K. Singh was to launch an assault on Turtuk on December 13/14 night. All necessary preparations were done; Rinchen and company were high and mighty prepared to assault.

The Dhal Force commenced their advance just after the last light to hit the respective targets. The entire advance was made under the cover of a mortar barrage. Several roadblocks of boulders and rocks were destroyed but Rinchen did not find any resistance coming forth from the Pak troops. At about 2200 hours, shelling was stopped and the troops advanced to Turtuk top village. By 0100 hours, they encircled the Wing, Headquarters and the village and charged with hand grenades and bayonets. Surprisingly, the village was lifeless and silent. It was pitch dark and no light was coming out of any house. No noise was heard except that of the dogs barking, donkeys braying and cows lowing. Every house was locked from within and despite all shouting, no one opened the doors.

At last, the Indian troops reached one of the big houses in the centre: of the village near the mosque. Rinchen knocked at the door with his stick and requested the inmates to open the door but there was no response. So, he posed as a porter from Baigdangdo and shouted in the Balti language, "I am Ali, a porter, resident of Baigdangdo. I come with the Indian Army but don't be afraid to open the door. The Indian soldiers will not harm you. I am responsible for your safety." It was after several efforts that finally there was a feeble voice from inside, "We are afraid of the Indian Army."

After great persuasion, two young men opened the door. Rinchen aimed his pistol at them and three jawans pointed their bayonets but Rinchen said politely, "Please don't be afraid of us, only tell us the truth. Is there any Pak soldier hiding in your house?"

They replied almost pleadingly, "Khudaki qasam, yahan koi Pakistani sipahi nahin hai." "Where are they?" asked Rinchen. "They have just run away after last light and the Pak camp has been dismantled", was their reply.

Rinchen's men entered the house and searched every nook and corner but found nothing suspicious. Only an old man, named Ghulam Husain and his two younger brothers, was found hiding in one corner of a room. He was a member of the village Panchayat and a rich man of the village.

As the members of the Rinchen's party were suffering from severe cold, they asked the inmates of the house to light a fire which they did but they were still afraid of the Indian troops. Rinchen talked to them in the local Balti language and tried to free them from fear, "Please do not fear, we have come to help you and free you from the Pak occupation after 23 years." Rinchen noted that while menfolk were present in the house, there were neither women nor children. He was told that all ladies and children were hiding in the adjoining Nullah for fear of the Indian troops. Rinchen thought it better to call forth the village Headman and Chairman of the Panchayat and take them into confidence. Lambardar Karim Mohammad Sang Sang and Ghulam Mohammad who arrived promptly invited Major Rinchen and his party to their house, 'Sang Sang House'.

Rinchen continued to plead, "Do not worry. I am an Officer of the Indian Army and come from the Nubra Valley." Immediately one villager recognised him, "So, you are from village Sumur and you are the son of Kunzang." Soon they gained confidence in what Rinchen said. Sang Sang served them nice Chinese tea in a China-made tea set. Rinchen asked the Headman and the Chairman who were political leaders of the village to call forth all the villagers at the Pak Camp at 0900 hours when he proposed to address them.

That was the moment Turtuk finally came under the Tiger's shelter, the balance of valour and compassion by Rinchen bestowed him the ability to win heart and battle simultaneously. The Turtuk victory turned out to be the liberation of a land from the hyena horde, about a thousand old and young people of Turtuk assembled to hear Major Rinchen. Everyone was carrying a white flag and shouting 'Hindustan Zindabad.' They also brought dry fruits and offered them to all ranks of the Indian forces.

In his address, Major Rinchen said: "We welcome you again to the Indian Nation after 23 years. The Indian Army will help you in all respects. Bring back your womenfolk and children. They are like our mothers and sisters. I will be responsible for their safety, if there is any misbehaviour on the part of any soldier or civilian who has come with us, I shall take disciplinary action against the person who misbehaves."

Further, he said "I want you all to settle down as free citizens of India. Visit your religious places, cultivate your fields, take out your cattle to the grazing ground and carry on your routine work as usual. India is a democratic country. Here people of different religions live and work together in peace and cooperation." Everyone was exceedingly happy to listen to the address given by Major Rinchen. They offered Major Rinchen the title of Nawab-E-Turtuk. The Tiger of Nubra was proclaimed as King of the village, the title he received was penned as his legacy nailed in Turtuk's soil eternally.

At 1100 hours, Colonel Udai Singh also arrived at Turtuk and the people received him warmly. December 14 was the victory day for the Ladakh Scouts and the Nubra Guards because on that day they captured the Pak Wing Headquarters on the Nubra Front. By 1600 hours, women returned from the Nullah along with the children, carrying bedding, rations, other necessary belongings, and small kids on their backs. All women had smeared their faces with black colour and mud, only their eyes were visible. On arrival, they washed off the pigment, returned to normal life and settled down happily. Rinchen learnt that the local civil population was suffering from a shortage of soap and salt. He immediately requested the Headquarters for the supply of the same. Three helicopters arrived bringing soap, salt, and rum: soap and salt for the civil population and rum for the soldiers.

By 1700 hours, Naib Subedar Angdus and his men also returned and reported that they had occupied the Pak post at Turtuk top and that the Pak forces had withdrawn along the Turtuk Nullah to the west.

Till now the laid strategy has come into proper materialisation by forces, the war has entered in third phase with new upfront objectives of the Indian troops were already on desk. First the troops were ordered to advance against Tyakshi, Pache Thang and Piun; and later they tasked to carry out hot pursuit of the retreating enemy forces to negate any escapees from the zone of sight.

Tyakshi village was approx 6 km from Turtuk and it was secured by 2100 hours on December 14. One of the Indian Army ambush parties succeeded in capturing Pak soldiers along with arms, ammunition, and other war equipment. These Pak soldiers were from the Gilgit Scouts and had come from Skardu to join as reinforcements. On the morning of December 15, Rinchen proceeded to Tyakshi and Pache Thang. Major S.K. Singh reported that Pakistan had offered little resistance and had withdrawn during the night towards Prahnu and Do Thang villages. According to him, while a few Pak soldiers were still crossing the bridge, one of them had been shot down by the Indian troops. At all the three villages, the people came out to receive the Indian forces as they had done at Turtuk. Major Rinchen addressed the villagers as he had done at Turtuk and assured them of the good intentions of the Indian Army. On December 15/16 night, they captured Thang and the Ridge which was later named Gorkha Ridge.

By the evening of 15 December, most of the Indian forces, comprising the Dhal Force, arrived at Turtuk. Some of the jawans represented that it was their New Year Day (Losar) and they were keen to celebrate it. Major Rinchen pointed out that it would not be proper to waste one day in celebrations when the enemy was preparing for a counterattack. He promised to celebrate Losar with great pomp and show, once the fighting was over. However, he got permission from the Commander for an extra issue of rum and a badakhana. He arranged with the local contractor, Mohammad Sang Sang, for the purchase of 12 sheep against full payment. The villagers made a free offer but Rinchen pointed out that unlike the Pakistani Army the Indian Army always liked to buy articles from the open market against full payment.

By then, the troops were quite tired and they needed reinforcement and replacement. One company of 5/3 GR arrived at Turtuk as reinforcement and to replace the wounded or frostbitten soldiers. Plenty of ammunition and ration supply was also brought in by the land route. One thousand ponies, yaks, donkeys, and porters arrived from the Nubra Valley bringing beddings which the troops had left behind at Baigdangdo. So far, the Indian troops had been virtually the guests of the Pak Army, using their ammunition, rations, and beddings.

A small force of the Ladakh Scouts, known as the Talwar Force, under the command of Captain S.D. Poon had left Leh sometime back. Advancing, along the Indus Valley crossing over Chorbat La, it was supposed to join the Dhal Force at Piun but due to failure of communication, their advances had been adversely affected.

By the evening of 15 December, Rinchen received a message from the forward Indian troops that Thang and Gorkha Ridge were completely under their control but the enemy was reported to be preparing defence at Do Thang and Prahnu villages. It was learnt that about two more companies of the Pak troops were arriving at their new defence line, presumably in preparation of a counter-attack. Rinchen ordered Major Thapa and Major Mishra (commanding 5/3 GR) who had reached the front on 17 December, to reinforce Pache Thang and Gorkha Ridge and to establish a base for launching an attack against Prahnu and Piun. The night of December 17–18 was fixed for the advance to Piun, unfortunately this could not be accomplished due to ceasefire establishment.

The news was received from the All India Radio that the Governments of India and Pakistan had agreed to a ceasefire at 1700 hours on December 17. A flash message was also received from the Brigade Headquarters ordering the Dhal Force to enforce ceasefire at the scheduled time. This greatly disappointed the troops whose morale was exceptionally high at that time and who were looking forward to liberating more of Baltistan including Skardu and Gilgit.

In this broad quest of war and weapons, Dhal Force has played the magnanimous role in shaping the course of operation laid by Indian Army. From the time that the Dhal Force had started from the Assembly Area at Baigdangdo on December 7 to December 17, when the forces reached Thang/Ridge, it had been almost ceaseless fighting for 10 days. During these 10 days' action, the Dhal Force, under the command of Major Rinchen and comprising exclusively the companies of the Ladakh Scouts and the Nubra Guards, achieved great success. Major Rinchen always recounts the important achievements on his fingertips. The unfathomable feat was achieved in this span of 10 days like, the troops captured Pt 18,402, which is the highest post ever captured in the world's history of warfare, later seized Chalunkha defence complex along with several villages covering approx 800 sq km. This was the largest area captured by any unit on the western/northern front during the 1971 war. During assault, several Pak soldiers were killed and many were taken, prisoner. A huge quantity of arms, ammunition and war equipment was seized, blankets and other clothing and rations were: captured in huge quantities. Blankets were distributed evenly among the porters. Rations lasted for many months for the troops. Not a single casualty occurred on the Indian side except for a few cases of minor injury and frostbite. Pakistani casualties included 18 killed, 2 JCOs, 40 ORs and 4 Razakars taken prisoner and six wounded who were taken to Leh by a chopper. Physical fitness and stamina of troops in ascending and descending the steep slopes of the mountains, along with arms and ammunition and some kit and bedding almost every night continuously from December 3 onwards was highly creditable. The troops still looked fresh and tough and were ready for the onward march. The entire operation was carried out without artillery and air support and with minimum expenditure of ammunition, using only hand grenades and bayonets. Most of the ammunition expended was captured from the Pakistani camps. This was grit of the force under Rinchen with minimal asset; zenith of feat was achieved like herculean tasks.

When, later, Lt. Gen. Sartaj Singh, the Corps Commander, visited and talked to the jawans at Turtuk he congratulated the Ladakh Scouts and the Nubra Guards on their bravery. He pointed out that there was not a single casualty because of good leadership, high morale, toughness, prompt action and adoption of high guerrilla tactics. While having tea in the crew room, Lt. Gen. Sartaj Singh pointed his stick at the revolver hanging by Rinchen's side and asked, "Rinchen, did you use this for the Pak troops?"

Rinchen replied, "No, sir, not this time. I only used hand grenades and Pak-captured ammunition against them." The General remarked, "Well done, Rinchen, you have saved our ammunition."

Later, the Ladakh Scouts battalion was granted the Battle Honour of Turtuk Operations of war. The forefront blazing claws of snow leopards under command of their tiger took the den of Turtuk within their shelter and under banner of India.

When a ceasefire came into force with effect from 1700 hours on 17 December, the exchange of fire from both sides on the fighting front came to an end. But lots of administrative problems cropped up. Once the conquests of war were successfully over, immediately the need for the conquests of peace was felt. It was a quest for the restoration of normalcy and peace at all levels. Rinchen's military exploits had been highly creditable winning, applause from everyone but he was not just a war-monger. Soon he became engaged in discharging his responsibilities in the aftermath of war.

The priority was, of course, given to setting up forward posts on the new frontier at Ridge and Thang by digging trenches and constructing sangars. This task was highly sensitive and needed to be accomplished promptly and firmly but very tactfully without violating the ceasefire and yet not yielding to external pressure tactics. On 18 December, when Rinchen visited the forward posts at the villages of Tyakshi, and Pache Thang, Lt. Bedi of the Gorkha Rifles whose platoon was engaged in digging trenches on the spur of a ridge reported that the Pak troops were trying to occupy more and more area. Rinchen advised him to deal with the situation very tactfully lest fresh confrontation flared up. He decided to send a message to the Pak Commander for a flag meeting and he also kept his own Sector Commander well informed about all developments.

Rinchen had firm command on his direction of belief regarding war and peace-giving virtue to his feelings which indicate how balanced his views are on matters of war and peace. He was conscious of the fact that the Commander of the troops should be not only accountable for success in war but also for all subsequent actions that were required to be taken for the restoration of normalcy. According to him, war should be avoided as far as possible. There is nothing good about war. It means so much bloodshed. It embitters relations between two neighbouring countries. It ruins the economy of both the countries involved.

"The winner wins the war but loses peace thereafter. But, if a war has to be fought, there can be nothing humane about it. One cannot be a softy. It must be merciless killing." But once a ceasefire is declared, the administrative responsibilities crop up manifold. The prisoners of war must be treated with dignity: the dead must be honoured and buried with full military honours and, above all, a lot must be done for the welfare of the people who have been liberated from the thraldom of the unlawful occupants to earn their goodwill. These were his ethics the reason he gained the trust of people and superiors whenever he took charge of some mission, even in neat uniform and badges of gallantry on his chest, his heart knew the true strength of compassion when he draws from the act of righteousness. It was his ethic's foundation on his entire fortress of manhood that stands with all dignity.

For him at a war you should fight with full intent, you can bayonet enemies during the war without showing any mercy. You are fully justified in doing, so. But once they surrender and approach you with hands up, they are your friends and guests. We can't arraign them for what they have done for their country, his moral stands on this virtue emphatically."

Proper burial of those killed during the war is another great responsibility of the Commander which he cannot afford to neglect. Rinchen detailed a team of Muslim jawans under a JCO along with a Maulvi of Baigdangdo to carry out all arrangements. It took five days to collect the dead bodies lying scattered all over the battlefields, select suitable sites for the burial grounds and then bury the dead according to their religious customs with full military honour.

Meanwhile, Rinchen had to tackle the immediate problems of the people who lived in the newly occupied territory. All the villagers from Tyakshi, and Pache Thang, including women and children, gathered at the school compound at Tyakshi and placed their immediate personal problems before Rinchen. In some cases, husbands and relations had been left behind on the Pak side. They had gone to Skardu and other places on business and many of them had been taken prisoner by the Pak soldiers while they were withdrawing. In certain cases, while the people lived in the villages on the Indian side, their fields and grazing grounds lay in the Pakistan-occupied area.

Knowing full well that these problems could best be solved by a flag. Meeting with the Pak Commander, Rinchen wrote him a letter in Urdu stating the problems and suggesting that a flag meeting be held the very next day and sent it to him through two messengers. Rinchen also informed his own Sector Commander about this proposal. Unfortunately, there was no response from the Pak Commander. The two messengers who carried the letter did not return. Rinchen emphasised the idea of mutual understanding in the region's development but the ego dipped men on Pak command shown no interest in joint humanitarian work, Rinchen neither hoped they will tag in this work but he understood that under his responsibilities. The village should get proper resources and development from all fronts. Nevertheless, Rinchen continued his work on Turtuk.

Rinchen also paid attention to the long-term problems of the newly liberated people. During the 23 years of occupation, the Pakistan Government had paid little attention to the improvement of the living conditions of the people in that area. Rinchen strongly felt that it was the bound duty of the Indian Army units to make the lives of the liberated people better and more comfortable.

There were many problems. There were a few primary schools but without teachers, there was no provision for fair price shops for rations and clothing; there was a dispensary but without a doctor; mosques in that area had not been repaired for long, and; above all, no funds had been allotted by the Pak Government for developmental work.

Immediate steps were taken by Rinchen to do something for the people in the liberated area to enable them to have a better standard of living and, indirectly, to earn their confidence and goodwill, he took charge for providing fair price shops opening for rations to be sold at subsidised rates, He made sure cooperatives were set up for clothing, kerosene, and other necessary items.

In addition, medical doctors and medical staff were posted at the hospital. Rinchen persuaded local people, though less qualified for employment, they were appointed as teachers in the primary schools. In the protection and administrative sector, he arranged a Naib Tahsildar and a Police Inspector to attend to the problems of revenue and law and order. Migration rights were bestowed on them; Permission was given to the local people to visit Leh, Srinagar and other places. Even financially, he looked after the allocation of special funds by the Army for the repair and maintenance of the mosques in that area.

Battles had been won with bayonets and grenades but providing a proper administrative system to the liberated people was a greater achievement for the Command. In true means, Turtuk was remerged in India after 23 years by bringing harmonious administrative efforts for local people. The legacy was inscribed at its very own on these battlefields when people supported the cause penned by Rinchen's effort and his beloved former Commander Col. Kapur's years back preparation and scaled prediction of liberating Turtuk from the enemy's clutches. Standing on a surveillance peak from the Turtuk side, Rinchen had a clear vision of the Partapur outpost.

He was remembering Col. Kapur fondly that day, Turtuk's siege was not a victory of his alone, somewhere it was dreamed by Col. Kapur and Rinchen made sure his former Commander's dream shall be fulfilled, The Tiger who freed these people and brought important sector inside the nation surely was crowned with the name of Nawab-E-Turtuk and in the Capital of the Nation, the gallantry of second MVC was waiting with his name on it.

❑

Chapter II

An Invincible Narration

16th December 1971

"Dacca (Dhaka) is now the free capital of a free country. We hail the people of Bangladesh in their hour of triumph. All nations who value the human spirit will recognise it as a significant milestone in man's quest for liberty."

- **Prime Minister Indira Gandhi in her historic announcement in parliament.**

Suddenly on the western front, a unilateral ceasefire was declared. The long impending war against Pakistan was over, favouring Indian victory and liberation of eastern Pakistan land with massive territorial changes coming with major shock striking at the heart of Pakistan's demographic shape. Indian forces captured around 15,010 square km of land in the West. Meanwhile, a new nation took its first breath under India's guidance in the east. The free state of Bangladesh was carved from several halves of Pakistan. That day, Indian Armed Forces reshaped the map of Asia and the world, bringing a new country on the desk of global seats.

Since World War II, this was the biggest capture of forces any nation ever did, clutching over massive 93,000 soldiers, one-third of the Pakistan Army surrendered on 16th December and blinked themselves as prisoners of war under the palm of the Indian Army. Lt. Gen. A.A.K Niazi, Commander of Pakistan Army Eastern Command raised the white flag with his forces and later raised the pen to sign the instrument of surrender, accepting the humiliated defeat on the face of Pakistan that day in Dhaka.

At the peak of the western frontier, under the summit of Karakoram and Baltistan region in Chalunkha sector, as the screaming and blazing symphony of war grew silent, a sound of natural airflow could be heard in an oddly silent atmosphere of Turtuk on Partapur front. This land which saw unsettled skirmishes for two decades in its rugged land was today in a a different phase with silence prevailed auspiciously in deep narrow gorges and ravines of inhospitable terrain, the region homes few hundred souls under the mercy of mountains living in several situated hamlets around this strategic bench, adjacent to stretched border on Karakoram-Baltistan lap of the valley across Chorbat La, the intriguingly raging voice of feet and fierce noise of movements somehow gone in silence. The sector for days loomed under attack and counter-attack disposition got its time in peace finally.

The Commander had his deepening visuals over some innocent faces, Major Chhewang Rinchen calmly cloistered his eyes onto few kids in arms of their mothers, this was his look of satisfaction on seeing locals safe since no innocent lives were jeopardised during battle, these villagers were scared and somewhat looking in hope towards these Indian men in uniform after capturing the sector to treat them with mercy. Rinchen's soldiers were setting up a perimeter around the region and making efforts to console and talk with the local men, as clouds of battle were faded with bringing sunlight of a new day over these people. It was a homecoming for them but with a basket of concern and fear on their head, since after two decades Turtuk was brought under Indian control, people of the land were reluctant to be convinced.

Sincerely, Rinchen took the charge to protect and talk to them personally. He gathered all people including women of the village and personally assured them that no harm will befall them and he shall take charge of necessary actions for the welfare and development of the people. In the same breath he ordered and directed his men towards the work and suddenly all faces in the village settled in satisfaction. The kindness shown by Ladakh Scouts and Nubra Guardsmen under the leadership of Chhewang Rinchen penned forth the preamble of trust in heart of these locals who finally made it back where they deserved, under the administration of the rightful nation.

The glimpse of the operation took a recap in Rinchen's mind as to how his men led this mission with a burning will to raid enemies in any given scenario. Acceptably Baltistan territory was very sparsely populated and the enemy posts were also not too critical to engage and raid but most of these were situated at dizzy heights adding little to no help from locals.

Major Rinchen took the battle at point 18,402, the grizzly and treacherous height of summit in that frontier at which no other battle has been fought in the military history of the world. The entire adventure of these warriors was untethered with no artillery and Air Force support and they had been on their own on those ruthless fronts. Rinchen and his men were resourceful with their determination to raid enemies to the core and through observation this operation was carried out with hand grenades and bayonets only. His base for maintenance support was fed by a precarious airlift to Thoise from Leh by old Packets.

The track right up to Turtuk was negotiated only on foot or ponies. As Rinchen's columns moved steadily forward, as if 'sucked into the vacuum', it is after the battle of Baltistan in which Rinchen had advanced about 22 km and occupied 804 sq km of enemy territory, there was a partial lull on the battlefront but complete dominance by the Indian Army. With non-detrimental settlement Rinchen assured to the people in the region; this led to the solving of the benign equation of locals' problem through Major Chhewang Rinchen's long-term posting on that bittercold outpost where he was stationed to safeguard Turtuk as the Western Sector Commander, with four companies of Ladakh Scouts deployed from Partapur to Turtuk under his command. By the end of the 1971 war, a sealed decree of gallantry was forged from his action to bring his second MAHA VIR CHAKRA on his proud chest.

When the news came in from HQ, the new sector commander remembered the predictive words of his senior officer Col. Kapur regarding the potential of his second MVC, the former Commander of Partapur boldly stated about this day and it was fulfilled by his own favourite soldier. His successor proved the mettle of his word and brought Turtuk under the waving flag of India. What is to be noted is the fact that not a single casualty occurred on the Indian side except for a few cases of minor injury and frostbite. On the Pakistan side, eighteen soldiers were killed and 2 JCOs, 40 ORs and 4 Razakar civilians were taken, prisoners. Huge quantities of arms and ammunition and other war equipment were seized. It is obvious that fighting on both fronts was conducted under the aegis of the same superior commanders, certain sharp contrasts in the conduct of war at lower levels resulted in heavy losses on one front and no losses on the other.

India stepped in the bright year of 1972 with a magnanimous victory over the enemy and it also brought Rinchen his gallantry award, Gazette Notification declared on 12th February 1972 for his second Mahavir Chakra.

The Citation for MVC Noted on Gazette:

"Major Chhewang Rinchen of Ladakh Scouts was commander of the force assigned the task of capturing the Chaunkha complex of enemy defences in the Partapur Sector. Each of these nine enemy strong points was held by one to two platoons and fortified with mines and wire obstacles. This operation was planned and executed with professional competence and great zeal. Under most adverse weather conditions, Major Rinchen led his command, displaying aggressive spirit and cool courage, fighting from bunker to bunker, exhorting and encouraging his men to destroy the enemy, making the operation a complete success. In this action, Major Chhewang Rinchen displayed inspiring leadership, indomitable courage, initiative, and exceptional devotion to duty in the highest traditions of the Indian Army."

For the second time in his service, Major Chhewang Rinchen was honoured with India's second-highest gallantry award for his valour in Operation Cactus Lily as it came to be known as later. With Bar to MVC, the Tiger of Nubra was bestowed with the hailing of "NAWAB-E- TURTUK" by his service mates and locals.

The brave NAWAB-E-TURTUK returned to his sector with profound responsibility to place Turtuk and Chaunkha complex into Indian administration and safeguarding the edges and posts from incursion by Pakistani forces since the Pakistani side was unacceptable of the conspicuous results of the war and resorting to misadventure on borderline. This was the time when the Indian Army held 93,000 Pakistani prisoners of war and negotiations were going on to establish a properly defined peace agreement by both nations, eight months after the 13-day India-Pakistan war ended on December 16, 1971.

Finally, both countries signed the Shimla Agreement under which India and Pakistan will recognise the 17th December unilateral ceasefire line as "Line of Control" in addition to releasing all 93,000 Pakistani prisoners of war (POW) the Indian Army had taken during the war after signing instrument of surrender. Rinchen and his garrison HQ knew this agreement won't be sufficient to stop Pakistan poking its nose and toe inside India's administrative region on the borderline. Major Rinchen remained on Turtuk sector as it was nonetheless a field assignment in a God-forsaken front area with lots of administrative and security problems, overseeing on this strategic post clustered on banks of Shyok river, Rinchen and his men were kept busy all the time in this complex settlement of villages.

The glory of Nubra's Tiger was on zenith, in his 24 years of ardent, determined and committed duty to India and 12 years of regular commissioned service to the Indian Army in Northern command surely made him an apex sentinel of Himalayas. But as the blazing and dazzling sun of noon sets into the horizon of abeyance in the evening, in a similar fashion the exaltation of Rinchen's persuasive career rumbled down at one point during his posting on Turtuk front when he realised his pending examinations regarding his ranking promotion, a sudden enlightening later pushed him to pour extra efforts to hustle for his promotion in rank.

The promotion process saw the hurdle due to series of given protocols of written attempts of elective subjects, especially through a set of promotional examinations Rinchen found hard to clear them and overall established regulations from which a permanent commissioned officer goes was mandatory for all military officers in posting. Despite having impeccable service records and being a highly decorated officer with two MVCs, one SM and one Mention in Dispatch, the rigid line of rules came to haunt Major Chhewang Rinchen after a euphoric day of receiving his second Maha Vir Charkra.

Perhaps the tiger's journey suddenly got into clutches of administrative dilemma where it slowed down his walk into a painful and annoying crossroad.

Now, the sector commander took the charge of four companies stationed in Turtuk, where his vigil began over sensitive passes and Trig Points junction through the newly recognised Line of Control (LOC). Ethereal flames of thought igniting in his mind, centred around a single standing question to himself "WHAT'S NEXT?" Anyway, it turned out to be an emphasised mystery for himself to solve, away from home, away from his parents, away from his wife and six children but mostly calmed under his work, his all sweats were poured towards his duty as his eyes set into utmost unitary focus for his responsibilities.

During his tenure as sector commander on the western frontier, he carried countless long deployment patrols to access the security of the village and measured the perimeter of the sector profoundly, ordered to put a routine for several teams to watch on strategic passages in the region under constant shuffle and he personally kept eye on enemies' activity beyond the line. The region was not fenced in any condition henceforth constant observation of adjacent routes and protection of outposts over strategic peaks were essential to him, no one was as exemplary than him in this part of Ladakh, his tactics for reconnaissance and surveillance were praised by his seniors in the pastime, now commander himself, he was no less than a Guru to his men, a cornerstone of deep treasured knowledge and military experience on the vast land of Ladakh, he raised Ladakh Scouts' young men under his command in excellent order.

Surely, he evolved as Sentinel of the Himalayan summit and carefully seeded Ladakh Scouts with his ethics and virtues under him, once a child of mountains today is hailed as protector of the Valley. He came a long way with his guts, high spirited will and true devotion towards his land and entire India. Despite living through such spine raising service and devoting more than half of his life to securing the nation's frontier, even an incredible officer like him needed to face the interior problems of the system; the promotional exams were standing as a wall between him and his ambitious destination.

His all active and passive senses were devoted to his duties for this long period of time, it surely made Major Chhewang Rinchen forget about certain prerequisites, which were essential in factor on his climb up on the ladder of his career, now it was bothering him, since his constant need on various post around vast

Ladakh region never allowed him to settle with the calm breath, not even in his hometown, serving from east to west frontiers all his life, he had a flickering amount of time for his exams, still, he managed to appear for his Promotion Examination time to time, his insurmountable hustle led him to clear Parts A, B and C before 1971 war. His real hurdle came with Part D.

Out of six papers of Part D, he had cleared three before 1971. In Oct 1972 he cleared two more; Administration and tactics with all his hard work. Only one paper in Current Affairs brought about all the troubles to him. In contrast, Current Affairs demand constant know-how about the world and country affairs and it needed supply of fresh incurred news and Rinchen was devoid of that facility in that part of the world, completely untouched from cities and busy inhabited regions like Leh and Turtuk he had neither newspapers nor magazines to deliver needed elements to Rinchen for preparation of Current Affairs.

At this point, anyone will assume that he was disinterested in the last paper and given a chain of studies to prepare. Seeing him, someone will say he might have been under the impression that he would get an exemption when the time comes due to his shining decorated service. Yes, he was hopeful that authorities might liberate him from this one paper and serve him his promotional badges on his shoulder, but he was never in false expectations. He kept giving his all heart and mind in efforts to bore him fruit in this endeavour he was silently going through. All his life, he never took a single thing for granted, whatever he received in his head, he honoured it with his pure virtues by living on his humble ground, such a resilient and straightforward character he was.

Since the early age of 17 he participated in wartime service, sacrificed his studies, and made himself available for the country on every given position through any given series of responsibilities, he was not even part of the Indian Army yet prevailed in his task through minimal resources available in major wars. Since 1948

Indo-Pak war, where he was been enlisted as Jemadar much against the rules, it was evident that how much his need was required on given gravitas of critical scenarios and it went on till the 1971 war, whenever the occasion was, Rinchen was called to safeguard Nubra frontier, be it against from Pakistan or China, he always responded the call without a sign of disobedience.

After the 1965 Indo-Pak War, following the advice of his superior Lt. Col. S.S. Randhawa MVC, AVSM, of the Ladakh Scouts, Maj. Rinchen managed to pass the Army Special Examination as early as 1966 but it did not help him in the search for his deserving rank.

Considerably this one paper has turned the edict for him, he never thought that one paper on Current Affairs could stand as a stumbling block between him and his clearance of the Promotion Examination. It deeply saddened him, the man who witnessed intolerable and treacherous days without conceding defeat was on verge of getting unexpectedly entrenched, imprisoning his single ambition to have its fruit. Same year on 24th October, Maj.Rinchen got a cherishing news, he and his wife welcomed their fourth daughter, whom they named Sonam Dolkar. Maj. Rinchen's family was happy with arrival of another child.

At his promotion struggle, Maj Rinchen after realising the evocative scenario of his case, he put a formal letter to HQ requesting for transfer from Turtuk to the Headquarters of Ladakh Scouts in Leh. HQ was unable to accept his request due to the importance of Ladakh Scouts presence in that sector, according to superiors the troops were not be acceded to because the enemy's hectic activities on the front and Rinchen knew this very well as he was witnessing enemies' mischief since the day, he assumed the role as sector commander. Enemies continued to bring fresh reinforcements around the clock, leaders of the Indian Army did not want to weaken the flank on that frontier since Pakistanis were making efforts to occupy places of tactical importance like the Trig Points on the LOC. Authorities trusted only Major Chhewang Rinchen for having vigil on the Turtuk front; he was considered to be the only Army Officer who could successfully tackle such sensitive situations since his expertise was unmatched on that part of the border. Saddened but not disheartened to deny his job, Commander of Western Sector, Major Chhewang Rinchen kept his morale high and continued to keep an eagle's eye on that strategic bench with his four companies of sentinels.

It was a blisteringly cold night of the year 1975 in December, the beloved commander was sitting alone at night beside a bonfire. Oddly it was a clear night with no snowy wind and blizzard mellowing on the land in winter. The sky was vividly enamoured with clusters of twinkling and beautiful stars. The Orion constellation was up ahead within the canvas of the universe. River of white stars painted in symphony in the middle of the sky, it was the Milky Way glittering up the heaven above. The harmony of quiet mountains with the dazzling sky was a spectacle to watch. Rinchen who silently looked at this marvel was holding a glass of rum and enjoying the view alone. For locals, it was a common sight even for Rinchen but it was like he felt the refreshing view of these stellar entangled jewels in the sky anew.

Rinchen's one junior saw him alone and walked towards him in curiosity. "Saabji!", he whispered.

Rinchen looked towards him and hushed "Speak, what's the matter?"

His junior replied, "It's nothing, just wondering what are you looking at for so long." Rinchen giggled and calmly said, "What you see up there, son?"

"Countless stars!" He replied.

Rinchen quotes further "Don't you find them amusing?"

Junior responds, "Agreed, but aren't they the same what we see every day? What is special about them today?"

Rinchen takes a few second pause and answers,

"The special thing today is that we gave our attention today".

He further adds, "Our life and duty for this land is also in the same case, it is common until we don't look to it, but the day we value it by giving our efforts, our observation and love, even this barren land turns incredible for us. This is the same land we call it mother since ages, we serve it without fail."

Junior says, "It's the wisdom of yours I am getting today".

Rinchen responds, "I'm reminding this to myself also, son. "We must do what is right, doesn't matter- the wave is against you, just keep going. Nothing can demotivate you; nothing can demotivate me till the day we are serving the right cause."

His junior smiled and replied, "Copy that commander, will remember this always." He walked away to camp.

Rinchen hushed again, seeing in the sky, "Nothing can demotivate me."

He still had looming thoughts about his promotion but even a brave Tiger like him needed the shelter of caring words and the remainder of his strength. Perhaps he was trying to see his reflection in those shining stars. A self-effort he used to make to keep his flame of determination high.

After ten months September 1976, his request was finally granted and he was posted to the 1 J&K NCC Battalion in Jammu, ending his long five years posting in the Turtuk sector. Even though he left Turtuk, he made sure people there shouldn't be deprived of basic necessity and behind his back, his successive sector commander would continue his welfare work in the village on behalf of the Indian Army, after posting in Jammu his hustle resumed and he appeared twice in the Current Affairs examination but failed both the times, his disappointment for this one paper was mounting on him, he continued to serve there until his reposting. In May 1978, he was transferred to Palampur as a Recruiting Officer.

During his service in Palampur, he got the heartbreaking news on his desk which he was not ready to receive. The beloved elder of Sumur village, representatives of the entire Nubra Valley community and Chhewang Rinchen's father Kunzang Dorje left the world. In his deep state of agony, Rinchen reached his village. United with his family and performed the funeral according to Buddhist customs. All his siblings were present including his younger sister. The mother of Nubra Jamyang Dolma was in the arms of his son during this hard day. Rinchen lived for enough days to settle his heart and mind, later he went to meet his wife and children before returning to his duty in Palampur.

After arriving there, he came to an understanding that his repetitive appearance for current affairs will not serve him any fruit for his effort; rather he thought to approach on special request for exemption of paper. Later he applied, through proper channels, to the Chief of the Army Staff for exemption from one paper of Current Affairs. By then he had put in 17 years' service as a regular Commissioned Officer and 31 years of total service in the military. The response by Chief was disheartening and completely shocking to him when he received a Director Order from the Chief of the Army Staff stating that it would not be possible to exempt him from that paper and he must go through the procedure to claim his Lt. Colonel rank.

His exertion was slowing down on fighting this battle with pen, seeing his disdainful look He was, later advised by the Chief to appear again and thoroughly request promotion as a special case. In his days of clouds, finally, sunlight peeked on him ending his long penance on the Current Affairs hurdle. At Palampur he was attached to 1 Guards where he came across to a kind-hearted officer, Major P.S Mann, who had just come back from the Staff College, after meeting Rinchen, Major Mann decided to get him through this maze and guided him deeply as a teacher and the day finally came when Major Rinchen got through the Current Affairs paper and cleared it. The man who knew the battle of rifle and bayonets finally managed to win this interior battle against exams with a pen, he wasted no time and took receipt of Part D result for formal submission. He addressed the Army Chief through proper channels for grant of Lt Colonel's rank with the attachment of the result sheet and receipt. The Army Chief Gen T N Raina had unfortunately retired by then and his advice to Maj Chhewang Rinchen was perhaps not recorded anywhere to allow Rinchen to have his deserving rank. The unexpected happened, General Raina's successor rejected his appeal with the remark that he had lost 7 years' service due to non-clearance of Part D within the scheduled time. This single statement made Rinchen give up on efforts to get the promotion; the decade of the 70s was nearing to end. Major Chhewang Rinchen turned 49 by then.

There is no second thought that after 1971, Chhewang Rinchen saw sad days on his slow journey during peacetime. After this last attempt went in vain, he felt totally demoralised and was silent for a few days. He didn't engage much in talks with anyone and one day he finally decided to go on premature retirement since it was futile to fight with an unending request letter to claim his promotion.

By then Lt Gen S.P. Malhotra had become the new Army Commander of Northern Command. He had commanded the 3 Infantry Division as the GOC during Indo-Pak War 1971 and had a positive approach towards Rinchen and was highly appreciative of the worth of Major Rinchen as a soldier. When news of Rinchen's premature retirement reached his ears, he personally came to Rinchen to prevent him from doing it. He tried to dissuade Major Rinchen from his plans to seek retirement, on several instances Lt. Gen. Malhotra tried to explain to Rinchen to change his decision but when Rinchen humbly insisted to release him from duty, his request was accepted formally and he was released with effect from May 1, 1980.

At the age of 49, Major Chhewang Rinchen retired from active duty in the Indian Army. He returned to Leh but before heading to his residence where he visited his mother in Sumur, spent a good number of days with her. Later he arrived with his wife and children.

His proven and undisputed fealty towards the nation and

Army had sealed inspiration for many soldiers, while retiring he was satisfied in the glaring notion of reality, he upheld the pride of the nation during his long tenure of safeguarding India's crown by watching every inch of Ladakh. Now the soldier returned to his den to rest but his responsibility was not over for his people in town.

❑

Chapter 12

An Endless Epic

A pair of old boots stomping and heading slowly on a known path, a slight rhythm of parade march could be felt. A mid-aged man with zero fatigue was on his way towards a village. The bright sun ascended the spot in the middle of the sky, it was sharp noon yet a blooming euphemism in the land could be felt, undoubtedly the captivating scenery could be tasted through the eyes of beholder who could cherish life. "NOTHING

CHANGES HERE EVER AND THAT'S WHY IT'S HOME!" he whispered. Few joyful old locals crossed the path with their Bactrian camels. He and the locals exchanged a moment of smile and continued on their path.

The man was Major Chhewang Rinchen who was heading towards his birthplace and hometown Sumur carrying a small backpack. It was June 1980, the snow was melting, green bushes waving near the banks of Shyok river downstream, sand dunes and clear blue dazzling sky were eager to identify his face. The child of Sumur was visiting his home for the first time without any service responsibility on his shoulder. His heart knew how he had felt when he kept his uniform and badges in his closet but somewhere he had hoped after such enduring service and beautiful penance in the duty of nation he might have a good start in his retirement days.

His hope was pure and righteous since he surely left the Army but the ethics of the Army never left him. The virtue of that 17-year-old young Chhewang Rinchen who led the battle and secured the vast land from the enemy's invasion was still bright and alive in his soul. His intent to serve people didn't abandon his will yet. Who would've been able to say after seeing his humble gesture that he was a war hero and legendary figure in Ladakh and Indian Army, for him and his people, he was just a common man with a kind soul who belonged to the terrain. His ways on the battlefield were unorthodox, unique, impeccable, and valiant but amid people, his ways were simple, modest, natural, and sincere which made him a soldier with a heart and mind once.

Upon entering the village, a plethora of greetings came his way as a son was getting warm hugs after his first school day. Eldest son of the village head Kunzang Dorje entered in the realm of his father's legacy, a minuscule but exquisite hamlet of few hundred people whom his father and he always cared about. Retired Maj. Rinchen who was visiting his ancestral home, to meet his elderly mother, had a permanent residency in Leh. His wife stayed back in Leh with their young grownup daughters and an 11-year-old son. After reaching home, Jamyang Dolma who was kindly revered as "Mother of Nubra" in the village saw her son on the doorstep and a brief spurt of tears gushed into her eyes when patiently she looked at him. She took her son in arms and welcomed him like he was a same 10-year-old child she used to adore in the early days before he moved to Leh. Major Rinchen might be a hero to his village but a gentle mother just saw her son who left home at a young age to follow his purpose and only returned in uniform morphing in the character of a soldier in front of her but later destiny witnessed what was penned down under the mighty summits of Nubra which changed the entire course of fate for the nation.

The wheel of time changed many things but not the heart of a mother. She couldn't accept the fact that she had her son in her arms again. The indomitable courage which was shaped in the field was fed in the womb of his mother.

Upon guessing his arrival, his dear sister and young brother rushed to home to see their elder brother for real which created a cherishing smile on Rinchen's face and for a moment he forgot the world completely seeing his family, but there was one person he was surely missing, it was his father. Kunzang Dorje was the pinnacle of inspiration for his eldest son; he had that gentle camaraderie approach that made sure an unbreakable bond should be established between his children in his absence. He stood by his son's side always; he was his comrade and buddy.

His legacy was materialised truly when Rinchen became a father figure to his younger siblings that day. He was always protective towards his younger ones, his responsible nature towards his family was stone inscribed truth in the home. Feisty and fiery in his outlook, Rinchen during his stay in the village took up the social cause to set up a store to sell basic commodities to help his younger brother who was once a part of the Nubra Guards. It was a one stone two fruit mission. He constructed a store in his village to accommodate the requirements of the village and helped his brother to be employed there efficiently.

Nonetheless, it was the time of the most auspicious festival of Ladakh, the Saka Dawa eve The gompa near the village reverberated the sacred chants at the first hit of the light in the morning. The horizon of Ladakhi ranges felt like calling skies to sing the gratitude of such a blissful day. Rinchen stepped into the village alleys to get a view around on a brightly lit morning.

While he was near the hilltop where his early childhood days got the joyous colours of fun and adventure, he saw a man of medium height with an affectionate demeanour was coming towards him. Chhewang Rinchen quickly recognised him, he was Havildar Tashi Motup, one of his intrepid and loyal friends who followed Rinchen in his long days of war. Havildar Motup served in Nubra Guards for years and was one of the close nonnos of Rinchen who bull charged with him on each event when Nubra Guards were called to the frontiers.

"It's refreshing once again to see you here, our Lion", Havildar Motup chuckled in exuberance.

"Such a lucky day to see you here, my brother", Major Rinchen responded.

"I heard you retired, Major!" Motup said.

"Yes brother, long 33 years of service, it was worth untie the laces of the boots", Rinchen smiled.

"We all followed your lead since 1947-48 war when you called us and raised Nubra Guards, feel like it was just yesterday", Motup said.

"I never expected it in such a glorified way, that in a mere matter of months I'll lead troops in war, but see how long we have come, it wouldn't be happening if my nonnos didn't support me", Rinchen replied.

"We trusted your guts; how couldn't we follow you? It feels like wartime is over now, since seeing you retired it feels like we are in peacetime again", Motup asked.

"I don't know brother, but my journey seems to be over here in the Army", Rinchen got a little saddened.

"I have a feeling, it isn't over, Major", Motup said.

"I have fulfilled all my responsibilities on that front, I have nothing there to head back," Rinchen hushed.

"Remember it was you who laid the foundation of defence for Nubra, it was you on whom we rallied behind, you led us and made sure our land remains intact, our gompa's remain safe from desecration, our women and children feel free and living", Motup reminded him.

"You never succumbed to defeat and you never gave up, I know your promotion got a hurdle which stopped you from going further but being the sentinel of mountains, this is not the end", He further added.

Humbly listening to Motup, Rinchen said "When the time will come Lord Buddha will show the way".

"For the time being, enjoy your retirement, Major", Havildar Motup laughed.

"Sure, I will do", Rinchen giggled.

Motup turned and started walking, in the middle of his way he stopped and took a pause.

"Every soul of Nubra knows, you are not the person who sits idle", Havildar Motup expressed the last of his words and walked away.

Rinchen laughed and whispered in his breath

"I WON'T, BROTHER, I WON'T!"

The clock turned when Rinchen decided to head back. Provenances of his current dilemma were hidden in his own mind; to prove them out he discovered the privilege to invest his time for social works in Leh. With that intent, he took the blessings from his mother, promised her that he would keep coming more frequently from now on to the village. With a bagful of memories, the lion of Nubra hit the road. Upon arrival to Leh, Rinchen sleeved up his efforts and not even a year of rest, he started focusing on various welfare works for the service mates in Ladakh. Chhewang Rinchen did not sit idle at home. The welfare of the service personnel was still close to his heart.

Before embracing his retirement plan in a complete official manner, Chhewang Rinchen visited New Delhi to enquiry about the procedure and proper directive channel to give a last try on his promotion case. Those days in New Delhi, Rinchen's relatives were staying there. One of his brother-in-law's brother, who was a security officer for the Dalai Lama before, had recently been posted in Delhi. Rinchen embarked and decided to stay there until he got final assurance from HQ about the status and chances of his promotion concluding his last effort and curiosity to settle.

Surprisingly the wife of his brother-in-law was second cousin sister to Rinchen's wife Chuskit Dolma, they had a son named Sonam Wangchuk. Sonam, 16-year-old, was studying in higher secondary school in Delhi. He got a reflection of his teenage days when he met young Sonam Wangchuk who was calm, sincere, respectful, and focused.

Rinchen had a wonderful stay in their home with them. However, unfortunately the Delhi HQ got nothing specific about his promotion and tenure extension. He sadly had to leave with no purpose to stay any longer, deciding to keep sticking with his retirement decision. He left Delhi for Leh, he bid farewell to his relatives and young Sonam Wangchuk.

Upon arrival at Leh, the tiger took up the dynamic social missions such as establishing an office in Leh to navigate and help people in necessary endeavours and for another three years, he took the bull charge of a diverse range of tasks to ease up the livelihood of people in his circle. Simultaneously, he raised his children with proper education resulting in his eldest daughter Phunsog Angmo becoming a great doctor and his younger daughter being a teacher, rest of his daughters were also raised with good education, his only son and youngest among his children took a deep interest in mighty Himalayan exploration which led him into mountaineering missions as a true Nubran inheriting his father's adventurous instinct. His Son Rinchen Wangchuk led his life in mountains and protecting its wildlife especially snow leopards, indeed he had tiger's heart like his father.

Rinchen never discouraged his children, he always kept imparting sacramental and humanitarian values in the life of his all five daughters and a son. Being a true warrior of the warfront and on the path of life, he made sure his all children carry a similar flame of will to live life in a great manner. He was an idol to many but as a father, he imprinted his own blood vastly by his virtues and wisdom.

Rinchen in his retirement days continued to take up projects to solve the problems of ex-servicemen, such as forming a Housing Colony in Leh called Ibex, setting up small scale industries or securing re-employment for his fellow ones. His known fellows used to come from long distances to seek help and guidance from him for countless problems. Rinchen got really swamped in his own house with the continuous arrival of guests and help-seekers. In a riveting scenario, Rinchen had established a discussion panchayat, his entire day used to be spent solving problems of needy ones, having a long walk-in city alley, parade ground and meeting his friends. For a long time, his stress and depression regarding being unable to achieve his promotion faded from his core of thinking.

For three years continuously, he made himself swamped in spectacle welfare tasks. By then he was blessed with a grandchild. Major Rinchen was now leading a common man's life, something every human aspires to seek, even a solid-thick serving soldier. He was contented in his present settling days. But fate had a different plan for the Tiger of Ladakh.

Major Rinchen's welfare services sang in a symphony that superiors in HQ heard his work with great appreciation. In September 1983, a silver lining appeared amid the passing clouds. Lt. Gen. Mohan Lal Chhibbar, then Army Commander, visited Leh. During his visit, he was warmly noted every development in the garrison, in midst of all the events, he felt something missing and uncanny. He later realised it was Major Chhewang Rinchen's absence that was disturbing him during the visit. Without deteriorating a fraction of second, he ordered the reports on Rinchen's case.

Upon realising the soundless yet throbbing struggle by one of his favourite soldiers, General Chhibbar sought to meet Rinchen the next day as early as possible. Rinchen's home was a kind of council for help seekers by then, it was amusing to see such decorated soldiers in different aura altogether. The atmosphere turned him the soldier into a social worker then. No wonder he loved to engage himself in something since his retirement, people used to come far from Chalunkha and Jammu to meet him. It was eye candy to see him still trying for his people with gentleness.

Visually it was completely surreal scenery, there was no need of jaw dropping expression about his current state. He was a people's man since his early days, the first impression anyone had about him was a human with an innocent smile and simplicity, nothing was big bearing and rough about him and his livelihood at the age of 52.

General Mohan Lal Chhibbar and Major Chhewang Rinchen had worked together. Major Rinchen served under him when Gen. Chhibbar had been the Brigade Commander at Tangdhar.

They both served in the Tangdhar post for a brief period, where Gen. Chhibbar took a great liking of Rinchen's soldiering ability, his uncompromising plus and sincere approach as an officer while commanding the troops. Rinchen's ACR report used to be thoroughly exemplary but the unfortunate rigidity of promotional protocols halted his dazzling service into a great peril of freezing.

Gen. Chhibbar called Rinchen to meet him in the garrison the next day. It appears that Gen. Chhibbar was not so bound by the 'book of rules.' He was more open-minded and large-hearted. He looked at the case from a human point of view. And it was a needed jolt of move since one of the highest decorated officers getting deprived of his right to promotion which was ethically and practically wrong. He deserved the promotion with utmost dignity after considering his unfathomable quality of service and his seniority in the Indian Army.

Major Rinchen readily agreed and went to HQ, where Gen. Chhibbar advised him to rejoin the Army. Major found this hard to grasp since it was more than three years since he parted his way from Military service. Later, when Lt. Gen. persuaded him to rejoin, Major Rinchen had accepted the proposal over the foundation of couple of demands in a matter of prerequisites he penned conspicuously. He put forth two conditions, one was home posting and the other one was promotion. Eventually, promotion was the cornerstone demand for resuming his service. Lt. Gen. Chhibbar empathised with Rinchen's consciousness for asking what he deserved in all way. It was not wrong but sincerely a full-fledged soldier like Major Rinchen realised his small noteworthy shortfall that ignoring Army's examination process during his hectic service on edges of border outposts.

His scenario made an enlightening mark on history that promotional process of military officers and gallantry decorations run parallel in their different charted dispositional ways, they occasionally cross each other in some path if fate rolled dices in fortunate way or we could say quite rarely.

Lt. Gen. Chhibbar. guided Major Rinchen through proper ways to achieve his promotion, Rinchen was asked to apply for MS-3 Army Headquarters through proper channels for reemployment, stepwise Rinchen obliged to the path charted by his senior and he did exactly the way Lt. Gen. said.

In the early quarter of 1984 at Ladakh Scouts HQ, Lt. Gen. Chhibbar was involved in an uncannily different task during his stay in Leh, his grandeur of action was unveiled when he authorised one of daring missions in the history of the Indian Army, away from all the occurring incident in Leh. In the steep north of Line of Control's last point, Pakistan Army was in untamed efforts to legitimise claim over the entire Siachen Glacier, Indian military planners identified the potential hostility and asked Lt. Gen. Prem Nath Hoon to execute a detailed plan to put the entire Glacier under Indian Army control with all three strategic mountain passes. Under the authorisation of Lt. Gen. Chhibbar and planning of Lt. Gen. Hoon, Operation Meghdoot was launched; the element of a spear to strike the world's highest battlefield was composed by entire Battalion of 3 Kumaon. Meanwhile, the units of Ladakh Scouts became the tip of that spear, since the mission was depending on their unmatched superiority in the mountain warfare and high-altitude operations. The 300 strong troops were led by Lt. Col. D. K. Khanna on the day of the Baisakhi festival.

By the end of 13th April, all three major mountain passes of Sia La, Bilafond La, and Gyong La with each strategic height of the Saltoro Ridge at the west of the Siachen Glacier were brought under India's control. Abundant resilience of the Kumaon Regiment and the Indomitable skills of Ladakh Scouts were properly used in the operation with the assistance of officers like Major R. S. Sandhu, Captain Sanjay Kulkarni and Captain P. V. Yadav who led different units on separate heights and executed exponential take over in a short time.

Rinchen's legacy laid in Ladakh Scouts. Since the inception of the force, Ladakh Scouts have come a long way to become a mature and capable regiment, led by the guidance of Major Chhewang Rinchen. Ladakh Scouts was created through merging of 7th Jammu Kashmir Militia composed of Nubra Guards and 14th Jammu Kashmir Militia on 1st June of 1963 under the command of Col. S.P Salunke. Chhewang Rinchen's Nubra Guards was a profound precursor to Ladakh Scouts.

Nubra Guard's operational tactics in blizzarding cold snowy mountains, survival instincts in treacherous sub-zero temperature terrain and procedures of high-altitude warfare were pioneered greatly by Chhewang Rinchen in the early days. It wouldn't be wrong to say that his legacy lives within every Ladakhi today who served in Ladakh Scouts and respectfully in other regiments. He is not just an inspiration to Ladakhis but every man who aspires to serve the nation on the border.

Back in Leh, to get an answer from HQ, Rinchen made his last ounce of his effort. It was a matter of great patience to get a proper response, Major Rinchen was not having any high hopes from the channel either but to honour the words and efforts of his honourable senior Lt. Gen. Chhibbar, Rinchen kept walking on the given guidance following all procedures. He put up his case for promotion based on being a highly decorated soldier in the Indian Army. Rinchen continued to explain his stand profoundly and formally through his request letter. Further, he aforementioned describing his seniority as a permanent commissioned officer since 1st June 1959 and the courses he had passed during his service. Rinchen left no stone unturned to give his ardent try to satisfy his heart for one last time since he had no expectations to get a positive response on his request.

After following the procedure, Rinchen waited with slim hope and kept doing his welfare work. He was immersed in his curriculum and family moments again. Occasionally he kept tabs and notes regarding the development of his case from garrison but he was well contained in his retirement days. His boon and blessing came in disguise as a storm to his gates after nearly one year of his formal application to HQ.

The auspicious moment unfurled in his life in August 1984, his penance was finally answered, by the Chief of Army Staff himself.

After several years of uncertainty, depression, and mental torment he had during clearing the complex series of exams and bearing no fruit to his efforts in the end, he was finally summoned to obtain his dignitary rank for which he had lost hope long ago. Under the surprised face, an old and patient officer was chuckling and cherishing the dawn of light he waited to see for endless days and nights. Major Rinchen for a moment rolled in his happiness which sprouted from his eyes in the form of tears.

His wife and children valued this news, his daughters and son celebrated their old man at home.

After a few days, the Chief of the Army Staff, General Arun Shridhar Vaidya, MVC and Bar, one of the highest decorated

COAS of the Indian Army, summoned Major Rinchen. He too was highly appreciative of the sterling and shining qualities of Chhewang Rinchen as a soldier, he decided to set aside the rules and regulations and asked him to meet him at the Leh Helipad during his visit to Leh Garrison.

The moment finally arrived, Major Rinchen was in ebullient spirit and yet composed enough to receive Gen. Vaidya at Helipad. Upon arrival when Gen. Vaidya saw him, he asked, "Why are you not wearing the badges of Lt. Col. Rank?"

Amused by his question, Chhewang Rinchen replied, "Sir, I have not received any orders so far."

Clearing his dilemma "You are promoted to the rank of a Lt. Col. and the orders were sent about one month back", was the reply of the General.

That clear statement by the COAS of the Indian Army himself made Rinchen take a deep breath before grasping the great news of his life.

The General came towards the newly promoted officer Lt. Col. Chhewang Rinchen, MVC and Bar, SM and shook his hands, greeted, and congratulated him in the presence of Lt. Gen. ML Chhibbar, the Army Commander, the man who was a reason behind this noble initiative, Lt. Gen. Hoon, the Corps Commander and Maj. Gen. Sharma, GOC 3 Infantry Division.

The Army Commander Lt. Gen. Chhibbar with great smile and satisfaction asked Rinchen to wear his rank thus assuming the position of Lieutenant Colonel. After five years of absence, the next day the Tiger of Nubra brightly came in uniform with badges and medals on his chest, seeing himself in a complete robe of promoted Lieutenant Colonel. The dream what he deserved come true after years of agonising hustle. Gen. Vaidya left for Delhi, before boarding his chopper, saluted and greeted his fellow officers on the ground.

Lt. Col. Chhewang Rinchen was one of the officers standing in line, saluting his chief with the same energy and might which he had 37 years ago at the time of assuming the rank of Jemadar in the war in 1947-48. After resuming his service again, then Lt. Col. Rinchen joined his duty at 246 Transit Camp, overseeing temporary residing soldiers presumed in the camp. For the upcoming days, he continued to serve in the camp where he received positively good remarks in his Annual Confidential Report favouring his next promotion and was recommended for the rank of Colonel after his three years of humble duty in the camp. But as it was being said, any greatest era of time would come to an end at some point, the sun had to set inevitably at dawn.

The extensive tenure of Colonel Chhewang Rinchen reached the destination of retirement, in September 1986 with full honour. Thereafter, he was posted with the Ladakh Scouts, with the rank of Honorary Colonel. During his childhood, he used to gaze at the parade ground where Military police troops came to train.

After retirement, spending his youth days in the field, seeing a few children at the same place where he used to stand in curiosity while looking at the troops parading on the ground that flashed his early childhood. From dreaming the day to living the same moment, his journey was an infinity.

Rinchen had kept looking at the kids in nostalgia when he heard a voice in his head, “Son, wake up!”, the voice was his mother’s, but she was nowhere in sight. Rinchen got puzzled, a few seconds later he heard again “My child, wake up!”, swiftly Rinchen opened his eyes, finding himself on his father’s rocking chair. His mother was standing beside him caressing his head to wake him up.

It took a moment but Retired Colonel Chhewang Rinchen realised he had been dreaming of his old times all night in slumber. A journey of many glorious decades got relived again in one single dream while he submerged himself in his nostalgia.

"Get up and freshen up son", his elderly mother left slowly after waking him up. "Yes, Mother", Rinchen said while rubbing his eyes and moving towards the bathroom to wash his face.

After having the morning meal with his mother, Rinchen sought to have a walk around the village again. Soon after he had crossed the threshold, he found some people were looking for him, they did not seem to be the locals of Sumur, Rinchen approached them and asked "I heard you people have uttered my name, how can I help you?", Rinchen's tone was obvious and stable.

"NAWAB-E-TURTUK, Rinchen", the bunch of mid-aged old men mentioned him graciously while folding hands in front of him.

Rinchen quickly realised they were locals of Turtuk village.

"It's a great surprise to see you, everyone, here, how did you people reach here?" Rinchen asked.

"We are coming from Leh, it is such a privileged moment for us to see you again", a Turtuk local told him.

"You all must have a long stressful journey I believe, come to my home everyone", Rinchen invited his old fellows.

"We are in peril, we came to seek your help and guidance on a particular matter", the man served his concern.

"Let's talk in my home, come everyone", Rinchen comforted each one of them subtly and kindly.

All local men who came to see him from Turtuk followed him, and the old tiger kept walking. The people around stood there just seeing him in grace and reverence.

The tiger might have retired from war and battles but he continued to serve his people till his last breath. It was hard for a tiger to stay just in the den when he owned a kingdom. He walked away from the sight slowly somewhere beyond the horizon; fading in the hazy scenery of Sumur.

Col. Chhewang Rinchen achieved the zenith of horizon once he desired to grasp. He ventured and led heroic events at the girth of various terra incognitas.

His legacy empowered every breathing soul of the valley; his service got inscribed in each beating heart of Ladakhis. Child of Jamyang Dolma and Kunzang Dorje penned his role as Tiger of Nubra, Nawab-E-Turtuk, Protector of Ladakh and Sentinel of the Himalayas in glory. He gave his heart for his nation, his whole life for the land and his love for everyone. The chronicles of Colonel Chhewang Rinchen, MVC and Bar, SM immortalised in these eternal summits of Himalayas through golden pages of the Indian Army's history forever.

Even today, the soil has the touch of his sweat and blood. The wind blows singing his glory. The mountains beget the sun with the rays of his courage. Below the green snow-covered land, there is an endless epic dozing off silently. When you happen to cross the Valley, assure that your heart hums lullaby of freedom.

❑

Endnote: The Legacy

Between the eternal summits of the Himalayas, the wind carries the symphony of his immortal name, his ode of valour, his echo of war cries, his deeds of righteousness, his service to the army and his love for the motherland. His four-decade glory from becoming Jemadar Chhewang Rinchen to kept his boots aside as Colonel Chhewang Rinchen, MVC & BAR, SM were filled with luminous moments that his life is a sheer reflection of an unfathomable journey where one can witness the endless warring sparkles with an amalgamation of harmony in them. Col. Rinchen's life is such an ardent inspiration to young generation that it has to be brought back on the desk to read and revive with the story of an unsung hero on whose courage the roads of Leh and Ladakh are laid. The painful and powerful anecdotes behind the entrancing land should be unveiled. To serve the purpose, we humbly encapsulated his high-spirited saga on these pages.

It is nature's law that every greatest soul departs to heavenly abode after marking his everlasting presence on earth and in everyone's heart through his valiant act. On Tuesday, 1st July, 1997, heaven gained a hero and the earth lost on. Col. Chhewang Rinchen left his beloved nation at the age of 66 years. He is irreplaceable. His deeds have been manifested in many souls today who serve in Indian Army with utmost pride. As India is railing towards modern times steadily, our tiger of Nubra left a safe haven for his upcoming cubs to evolve and emerge under the summits in tranquillity. For us, this is his supreme legacy he ever created to mention before the rise of prominent Ladakh Scouts Aka Snow leopards whom today world knows as the elite mountain warfare unit.

The young 16-year-old Sonam Wangchuk we saw in Endless Epic went on to write his own legendary journey ahead in the Kargil War by earning a MVC on his name himself. He is none other than Colonel Sonam Wangchuk, MVC, Hero of Chorbat La and Lion of Ladakh. Col. Sonam Wangchuk got inspiration from Col. Rinchen and Col. Wangdus to join army, Col. Sonam Wangchuk joined Indian Army through OTA as Second Lieutenant in 4th Battalion of Assam Regiment, he served in the north-eastern sector as Company Commander and went to serve in Sri Lanka in Indian Army Peacekeeping Force. By outbreak of Kargil War, Col. Sonam Wangchuk was already a Major while serving in Indus wing of Ladakh Scouts. In Kargil war, he led a daring successful operation on Chorbat La axis, hailed as first successful mission in Operation Vijay, that event was foundation of Indian Army's successful retaliation against Pakistan Army's wicked invasion in Kargil. His heroic act earned him Mahavir Chakra in Kargil War. He is a shining legacy of Col. Chhewang Rinchen's efforts to raise warriors of Ladakh in Indian Army. After long and dauntless service to army, Col. Sonam Wangchuk is happily retired from service and continues to be great inspiration to youngsters, encouraging future generations on the line of great ethics and principles as he himself is an embodiment of such gallant way of life.

After his departure, Col. Rinchen's ancestral home, the fame Stakre House was converted into a heritage site for locals and tourist attraction. The site was inaugurated by Lt Gen. Y.K. Joshi, on October 5, 2019 at his hometown Sumur, Nubra valley. The project was taken by 'Tejasve Teen' battalion of the Ladakh Scouts Regiment under the aegis of the Fire and Fury Corps, with the guidance of Lt. Gen. Y.K. Joshi who then served as GOC in C of Fire and Fury Corps. The Sumur village itself is an epitome of Col. Rinchen's history, a momentous witness to his life. To our surprise, even today, away from his village at one strategic pass some bike riders, who know the legend, remembers him while drinking tea and coffee. Worlds highest cafeteria was named after Col. Chhewang Rinchen, at the height of 18,360ft, Rinchen Cafeteria sits along the Khardung La Road, which is one of the highest motorable roads in the world. The cafe is maintained by the army and its a major attraction on the way of high road travels in Ladakh, a photogenic cafe with savory breakfast and piping hot beverages dons the name of Nubra's tiger.

Like every subtle thing, the Shyok River, too, has its fair share of stories in the heroic journey of Col. Rinchen. In October 2019, Indian Defense Minister Rajnath Singh inaugurated the worlds highest all weather permanent bridge named after Col. Rinchen, also known as Col. Chhewang Rinchen Setu. The bridge's superstructure is called 'Extra Wide Bailey Bridge' and It was constructed by Border Roads Organisation in record 15 months. It is located in eastern Ladakh at nearly 45 km from the country's border with China. The bridge holds strategic importance for its ability to connect the entire Leh with Jammu and Kashmir, bringing critical pass within the network of Indian roads. The bridge connects Durbuk and Daulat Beg Oldie areas. It is a section of the road between Karakoram Pass and Leh region. The 400-meter-long strategic bridge is situated at a height of 14,650 feet. Col. Rinchen and his young band of Nonnos knew the land as their back of hand back in early days, naming a strategic bridge after him was a reminder to everyone including the adversaries that once lived a legend and his spirit still serves the nation.

While listening and writing his life, the incidents and anecdotes took us back to his life. There was a burst of emotion, courage, willpower, harmony, and wisdom while hearing his life in minute details, he encompasses a complete life journey, like a saint with sword, bravery in eyes but compassion in his instincts. His legacy cannot be encapsulated with details as he dwells in hearts of many without a loud bang. His vibe revolves around and it lies in each soul, today, who ignites the flame of courage to travel through the roads to reach their post to guard the nation. It is our extreme craving and wish to carve his name in more young hearts so they can travel to witness his legacy in the Himalayas where his name can be heard resonating in the summits even today and will continue to be echoed forever and propel to follow the legacy of serving our nation.

Even if we are able to connect, at least, ONE heart to the core of his story and manage to bring him closer to the mainland of our nation and the true essence of Indian Army then we will consider our penmanship is worth it.

A SOLDIER NEVER PERISHES, NOR HE CAN BE FORGOTTON.

Their sword and rifle will always be remembered through our pen.......... JAI HIND!

❑